11 January 2006
Stan Allen
*Strategies
and Tactics*
Evening lecture

12 January 2006
Cristiano Ceccato
*On Generative
Form-finding and Parametric
Rationalisation for Constructability*
Evening lecture

12 January 2006
Gehry Technologies *Digital Project
Software*
Start of two-day open workshop with
Edoardo Luzzatto-Giuliani, Djorje
Stojanovic and Charlie Maguire

13 January 2006
Pascal Schöning:
Cinematic Architecture
Mari Mahr:
Daughter of an Architect
Exhibition openings and book launch
for Manifesto for a Cinematic
Architecture

16 –18 January 2006
Andrew Benjamin
The Image of Architecture
Evening lecture

17 January 2006
Sébastien Marot
*Palimpsestuous Ithaca:
A Relative Manifesto*
Evening lecture

17 /18 January 2006
Andrew Benjamin
*I Modelling Architecture
II Displaying Architecture*
Visiting theory seminars

18 January 2006
Sarah Whiting
Looking Good
Evening lecture

19 January 2006
Diploma School Open Evening

19 January 2006
Jesse Reiser
Projects and their Consequences
Evening lecture

19/20 January
Sarah Whiting
Architecture's Social Imaginary
Visiting theory seminars

20 January 2006
Georges Didi-Huberman
Image, Event and Duration
Artist series
Chaired by Michael Newman

24 January 2006
Hernan Diaz-Alonso
The Grotesque and the Horrific

In conversation with Brett Steele
25 January 2006
Axel Kilian
Advanced Digit...
Open lecture

26 January 2006
Ali Rahim
Catalytic Forma...
Evening lecture

26/27 January 2006
DRL Phase II Final Jury:
'Create Space'
Invited critics
Mark Burry
Ali Rahim
Zaha Hadid
Marta Male-Alemany
Hernan Diaz Alonso
Florencia Pita
Benjamin Bratten
Warren Neidich
Kieran Long
Lucas Dietrich
Ranulph Glanville
Bob Lang & others

27 January 2006
Graduate School Open Day

27 January 2006
Mark Burry
*Antoni Gaudi and
the Status of his
Drawings and Models*
Evening lecture

30 January 2006
Peter Eisenman + Rem Koolhaas
In Conversation
Moderated by Brett Steele

30 January 2006
*Still: images from the film archive of
the AA Photo Library*
Exhibition opening

31 January 2006
Cynthia Davidson
*An Introduction to Log:
Observations on Architecture and
the Contemporary City*
Visiting theory seminar organised by
the Architectural Urbanism, Social &
Political Space Research Cluster

1 February 2006
Jeff Kipnis
Robert Somol
On Koolhaas + Eisenman:Two Views
Evening event

2 February 2006
James Corner
Thick
Evening lecture

3 February 2006
Thomas Demand
Artist series
Chaired by Parveen Adams

6 February 2006
Paolo Papale and Jacques Durrieux
Seismic Extremes
Open lecture hosted by Diploma 16

*...he Space Producer'
...el Dissected and
...al)*

...**pen Juries**

9 February 2006
Mari Mahr
Daughter of an Architect
Evening lecture

10 February 2006
Catherine du Toit
*LAB06 Student Festival/
AA Social Cinema*
Open workshop for students across
the School

10 February 2006
Parveen Adams
*Hung, Drawn & Quartered, or Goya
after the Chapmans*
Artist series
Chaired by Simon Baker

14 February 2006
David Adjaye
Making Public Buildings
Evening lecture

16 February 2006
Bas Reedijk + Deepak Vatvani
Seismic Extremes II: Tsunami
Open lunchtime lecture

17 February 2006
Toyo Ito
*Morning conversation
with AA students*
Moderated by Shin Egashira and
Brett Steele

17 February 2006
Tony Vidler
Open theory seminar chaired by
Mark Cousins

17 February 2006
Taira Nishizawa
*How to Create the Contemporary
Architecture*
Lunchtime lecture

17 February 2006
Christian Marclay
Artist Series
Chaired by Mark Godfrey

17 February 2006
Madelon Vriesendorp
Enigmatic Signifiers
Exhibition opening

20 February 2006
Alisa Andrasek
*Material Potency: Probablistic
Programming: Emergent
Composure: Polyscale*
Evening lecture

Timeline continues inside back cover

D0890456

AA Projects Review 05/06 has been produced
through the AA Print Studio by Rosa Ainley,
Clare Barrett, Pamela Johnston, Nadine Rinderer,
Marilyn Sparrow and David Terrien.

© 2006 Architectural Association

ISBN 1 902902 50 5
978 1 902902 50 0
ISSN 0265-4644

Printed in England by Dexter Graphics Ltd
Thanks to Eric Olson (processtypefoundry.com)

AA Projects Review 05/06 and back issues
are available from AA Publications,
36 Bedford Square, London WC1B 3ES
publications@aaschool.ac.uk
aaschool.ac.uk/publications

Cover: Plan of the AA Summer Pavilion, designed
and manufactured by Intermediate Unit 2 at
Hooke Park and erected in Bedford Square, June
2006, with the generous assistance and support of
Finnforest UK, Maeda Corporation, Arup AGU
and Architen Landrell, as well as media sponsor
Building Design. Drawing by Simon Whittle,
Intermediate Unit 2.

Experimentaation
The AA, 2005/06

The AA is exactly what its name proclaims: an association, of a decidedly architectural kind. It is this word, association, which I believe provides a concise indicator for how the AA will confront the challenges of our time: by choosing to actively explore how we wish to associate ourselves, not only within the different parts of the School, but also within the larger world in which we are situated. The advent of information economies, global travel, high-speed networks and constantly evolving communication technologies has brought an end to the era of supposedly 'autonomous' architectures – of making 'architecture about architecture'. Today architecture has much to learn from, and share with, a broad range of other creative disciplines and cultural activities. Our generation is already being shaped by (and may ultimately be defined through) how we negotiate the complexities related to the associative realities of our world.

2005/06 has been a year in which the AA has begun confronting this challenge, both internally, in how we choose to organise our activities, as well as beyond our walls, in how we work with others. This past year has seen the launch of new research clusters that define broad, but clearly delineated, forms of architectural knowledge, through which different units, programmes and external collaborators can come together for debate and exchange. We have also redesigned our First Year pedagogy as an open, collaborative studio instead of isolated units, allowing our youngest students and a great team of tutors to explore what it means to initiate an architectural education today.

To these changes we have added a new series of open theory seminars with renowned architectural theorists and critics that have attracted great interest from across the entire School. I'm very pleased that our exhibitions and publications have featured much more the work of our great students, ex-students and teachers, allowing them all opportunities to share their work with large audiences. Our two major conferences this year were organised in collaboration with outside institutions including other schools and offices. The agendas of our many units and programmes have, as is often the case, created yearlong associations with countless external settings and collaborators.

Locally, our students have worked within the immediate context of London on projects that have engaged with the Greater London Authority, the redevelopment of King's Cross, the rapidly developing landscape of East London and the Thames Gateway, the complexities of the NHS and the large-scale developments of White City and Stratford City. The rapidly changing conditions of London make it an unparalleled urban laboratory for so many parts of our School.

Alongside these projects, our international student population has addressed problems related to geographies as diverse as their own origins, completing projects for Panama City, Iceland, Kowloon, China and many other locations. During the year, our students and tutors have covered the globe, lecturing, presenting and researching projects at host schools and other institutions in Tokyo, Shanghai, Sri Lanka and Mexico City. While our students have taken their work out into the world as an essential part of their studies, we in turn have welcomed to Bedford Square a steady stream of the world's leading architects, theorists and artists, as part of our ambitious programme of public events and activities. The following review is intended to offer a brief glimpse into our life this past year, which we have chosen to title 'Experimentaation'. We all look forward to pursuing the experiment further next year.

Brett Steele
Director, AA School of Architecture
director@aaschool.ac.uk

From top: The Year(s) Ahead, AA Director Brett Steele addressng the Architectural Association, November 2005; AA First Year studio now; AA students in the same space in the 1950s.

Left to right, from top: Lars Spuybroek, 'Machining Architecture', Evening Lecture, 12.10.05; Francois Roche, 'R&Sie(n) Architects', Evening Lecture, 14.03.06; Zaha Hadid, 'The Design of the Phaeno Centre', Evening Lecture, 28.02.06; Ed Soja, 'Mesogeographies: Urban Spaces in a Regional Age', Evening Lecture, 06.12.05; Winka Dubbledam, 'From Hardware to SoftForm', Evening Lecture, 15.03.06; Peter Eisenman & Rem Koolhaas, In Conversation, 30.01.06; Detlef Mertins, 'Goodness Greatness: The Image of Mies Reconsidered', Evening Lecture, 20.10.05; Eric Owen Moss, 'In Sight of the Invisible', Evening Lecture, 06.03.06 (photos Valerie Bennett).

Left to right, from top: Toyo Ito, Morning Conversation, 17.02.06; Anthony Vidler, Open Theory Seminar, 17.02.06; Jeffrey Kipnis & Robert Somol, 'On Koolhaas & Eisenman: Two Views', Evening Lecture, 01.02.06; David Adjaye, 'Making Public Buildings', Evening Lecture, 14.02.06; Thomas Demand, Artist Talks, 03.02.06; Charles Jencks & Paul Finch, 'The Iconic Building: A Transitory or Permanent Condition?', Evening Lecture, 23.02.06; Hans Olrich Obrist & Stefano Boeri, In Conversation, 10.03.06; Alisa Andrasek, 'Material Potency', Evening Lecture, 20.02.06 (photos Valerie Bennett).

Left to right, from top: DRL Phase I, Architecta, December 2005; School Meeting, November 2005; AA Independent Radio: Runzelstirn & Gurgelstock/Schimpfluch Gruppe, May 2006; Fifth Year Previews, May 2006; Undergraduate Jury Week, Dip 13 Jury, June 2006; Dip 2 Jury, June 2006; queuing for Zaha Hadid's lecture, March 2006; Intro Week, First Year Studio presentation, October 2005 (all photos but top left Valerie Bennett).

Left to right, from top: Environment & Energy meeting with Simos Yannas, June 2006; Mark Cousins in his office, June 2006; AA Workshop, June 2006; Intermediate School Introductions, Inter 3, October 2005; DRL Phase II Final Jury, January 2006; Dip 14 at work in the AA Bar, February 2006; Diploma School Introductions, Dip 1, October 2005; fireworks from the terrace, Bonfire Night, November 2005 (photos Valerie Bennett and Rosa Ainley).

Left to right, from top: Opening night, 'Still', AA Photo Library, March 2006; opening night, 'Plasma Studio', AA Gallery, November 2005; opening night, 'Caruso St John: Cover Versions', AA Gallery, October 2005; 'AA Diploma Honours Students 2004/05', Front Members' Room, October 2005; Intro Week, AA Dinining Room, October 2005; First Year Jury, February 2006; opening night, 'Phaeno Science Centre', AA Gallery, February 2006 (photos Valerie Bennett and Chris Fenn).

Left to right, from top: Opening night, 'Cinematic Architecture', AA Gallery, January 2006; opening night, 'Thames Gateway Assembly at the AA', AA Gallery, April 2006; 'Teacher/Student: Not the Last Word' exhibition, Front Members' Room, March 2006; 'Mari Mahr: Daughter of an Architect' exhibition, Front Members' Room, January 2006; Research Cluster meeting, November 2005; Morphogenetic Design Symposium, March 2006; Surface Intelligence: Ambient and Augmented Architectures symposium, November 2005; Open Jury Week, February 2006 (photos Valerie Bennett and Sue Barr).

First Year Studio, Regent's Park Mapping
Project, May 2006 (photo Valerie Bennett)

Foundation and First Year

Foundation

What's Cooking?

1. Menu
The first project introduced the students to the notion of food as a representational medium with the design of a personal menu both in 2d and 3d. The menus encapsulate each individual in terms of personality, culture, environment and creative desires.

Antipasti
Following the introductory menu the students began a series of starters exploring food and its consumption in relation to different scales of space within the city.

2a. Domestic Space
Survey of personal living space and the ways in which these spaces are used – eating habits, movements between rooms and the temporal cycles of domestic space. Measured survey drawings, sequential photographs and time and movement diagrams.

2b. Public Space – London Picnic
Survey of urban spaces. Mappings of journeys between home and a particular location in London for a picnic. Picnics designed in response to each individual journey and location.

2c. Public Space – The Third Place
The chosen picnic sites transformed with the design of a culinary event exploring the space between the public and the domestic (the third place).

Primi
3. Cooking and Construction
Edible item examined in order to discover form, structure, space, mechanisms and the transformative properties of the 'material' as well as its place in the cultural network. Explored through analytical drawing and modelling.

4. Consuming Space
Video project exploring the cultural and spatial in relation to 'consumption'.

Secondi
5. Eat/ Live/ Show
The final event was the result of an exploratory and evolutionary process. Students designed performative culinary structures that are demountable and adaptive to a number of conditions. The prototype at 1:1 explored the interface with the body, as an applied device.

Dolce e Caffe
Projects Review café lounge

Unit Staff: Miraj Ahmed, Saskia Lewis, Theo Lorenz

Students: Nadiah Ahmad Nazri, Anna Andrich, Tala Fustok, Friedrich Gräfling, Matthew McNelly Jones, Jin-Ho Kim, Alexia Kouzeli, Ji Hyun Lee, Jin-Kyu Moon, Rama Nshiewat, Lambros Serghides, Wen Ying Teh, Seung Hyun Yuh

Workshops: Amr Assad, Sue Barr, Mark Tynan, Dr Tanja Siems, Carolin Hinne, Takako Hasegawa, Joel Newman, Nogal Zahabi

Thanks to: AA Workshop team, Sabrina Blakstad, Teresa Cheung, Marilyn Dyer, Tom Emerson, Nate Kolbe, Andreas Lang, Antonia Loyd, Brett Steele, Anna Sutor, Peter Staub, Toby, Dino Rossi, Simone Sagi, Martina Schäfer, Valentin Bontjes Van Beek, Charlie and Georgie Corry Wright

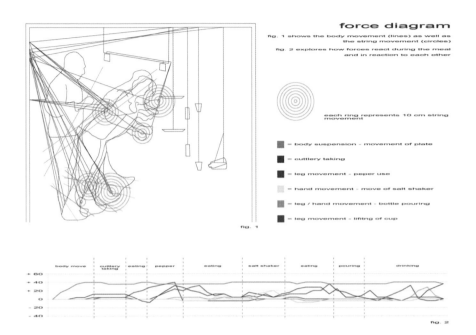

force diagram

fig. 1 shows the body movement (lines) as well as
the string movement (circles)

fig. 2 explores how forces react during the meal
and in reaction to each other

each ring represents 10 cm string
movement

■ = body suspension - movement of plate

■ = cuttlery taking

■ = leg movement - peper use

■ = hand movement - move of salt shaker

■ = leg / hand movement - bottle pouring

■ = leg movement - lifitng of cup

fig. 1

fig. 2

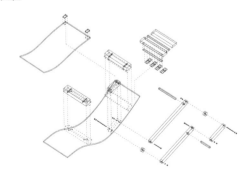

Above and right: Friedrich Gräfling
Friedrich's project is about suspension.
The process of eating is extended – suspended
through the use of elasticated cables attached
to the body and to food.

Below: Jin-Ho Kim
The starting point of Jin Ho's project is
cultural difference, identifiable in the posture
of the body while eating. An adaptive piece of
furniture was developed to explore specific
eating positions.

Project 5 - phase 1 ; Live / Eat / Show

PROCESS
A STUDY OF MAKING THE 2D PLAN TO A 3D MODEL

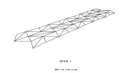 

STEP 1
SET UP THE PLAN

STEP 2
FOLD EACH TRIANGLE FOLLOWING THE DIRECTIONS

STEP 3
ROLL UP THE EDGES OF THE PLAN

STEP 4
CONNECT THE EDGES AND A MODEL IS COMPLETE

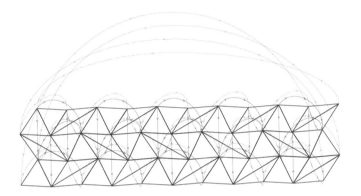

Above and left: Seung Hyun Yuh
Seung became interested in the transformation of shape in the consumption of an apple
and explored the idea further in the design of a
flexible structural form that changes according to the 'consumption' of space within.

Below: Rama Nshiewat
The cultural importance of eating with the
right hand became the basis for a performance
installation highlighting the ergonomics of
dining and the various interfaces with the body.

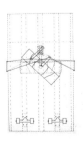

Anna Andrich
Cyber Flirting
Anna's exploration of non-verbal
communication at social dining
events led to the design of
electronic body extensions for the
purpose of flirting.

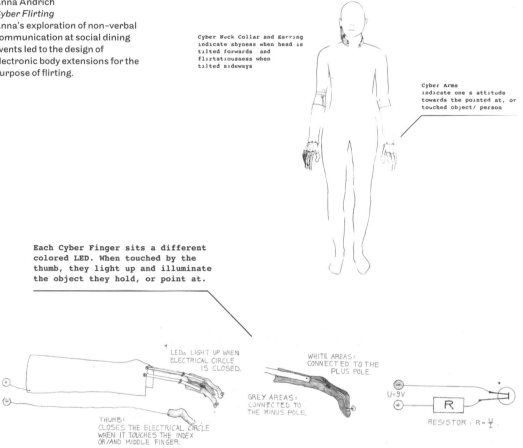

Cyber Neck Collar and Earring
indicate shyness when head is
tilted forwards and
flirtatiousness when
tilted sideways

Cyber Arms
indicate one s attitude
towards the pointed at, or
touched object/ person

**Each Cyber Finger sits a different
colored LED. When touched by the
thumb, they light up and illuminate
the object they hold, or point at.**

LEDs LIGHT UP WHEN
ELECTRICAL CIRCLE
IS CLOSED.

WHITE AREAS:
CONNECTED TO THE
PLUS POLE.

GREY AREAS:
CONNECTED TO
THE MINUS POLE.

THUMB:
CLOSES THE ELECTRICAL CIRCLE
WHEN IT TOUCHES THE INDEX
OR/AND MIDDLE FINGER.

U=9V

RESISTOR: $R = \frac{U}{I}$.

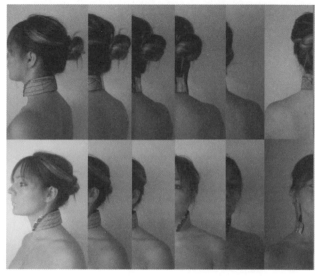

First Year Studio

The new First Year structure aimed at allowing a body of students to intermingle and diversify, and broaden the base of their education. A central focus was to ensure that each student sampled a range of techniques for the production of architecture, starting with simple, separate skill-sets before broadening into larger questions around the values and distinctions of architecture, and then choosing their area of concentration.

The year began with a journey through 2-, 3- and 4-dimensional thinking. Whether notating and transforming a range of patterns, constructing an augmentative prosthetic for the body or re-specialising the body of the School through video. Drawing led to models, spaces led to films, moving images led back to drawings.

In the second term students tested the boundaries of architecture with a series of installations across the School, whether rewiring and purposefully overloading the lighting circuitry, ensnaring the ceilings with barbed wire clouds, running hot water through the terrace railings or wrapping wheeled furniture in bubble wrap, projects tested an impact on spaces. The next three weeks, spent drawing fridges, complicated basic drafting skills with the realisation that mere delineation of form would fail to capture their fundamental essence.

Analysis ceded to intervention and proposition in the second and third terms as students studied larger, urban fridges (aka supermarkets) before remixing and suturing them and their apparatuses onto sites in and around Regent's Park. Having clambered around the musical scale and played a number of instruments, they finally focused on a specific brief around this common theme, honing their final composition. On the floor of our studio, a room-sized 1:200 communal drawing of the park, oriented to north, suggested First Year's walk in the park.

Thanks to: Miraj Ahmed, Manuela Antoniu, Rubens Azevedo, Claude Ballini, Larry Barth, Kathrin Böhm, Katharina Borsi, Asa Bruno, Reem Charif, Fergus Comer, Michel da Costa Goncalves, Daniel Dendra, Oliver Domeisen, Tom Fecht, Alistair Gill, Ben Godber, Annika Grafweg, Samantha Hardingham, Cathy Hawley, Mariana Ibanez, Simon Kim, Olaf Kneer, Nate Kolbe, Andreas Lang, George L Legendre, Monia de Marchi, Markus Miessen, Mike Mitchell, Matthew Murphy, Yusuke Obuchi, Anne Save de Beaurecueil, Janek Schaefer, Pascal Schöning, Ro Spankie, Stephen Roe, Janek Schafer, Veronika Schmid, Goswin Schwendinger, Charles Tashima, Jose Tovar-Barriendos, Carlos Villanueva Brandt, Chiafang Wu, Simos Yannas

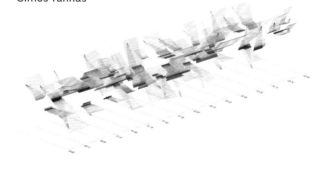

Valentin Bontjes van Beek	Azri Syazwan Abdul Gani
	Sanem Alper
	Kim Diego Alvarez Barreiros Azevedo
	Umberto Bellardi Ricci
	Ai Bessho
	Flavie Colliac
	Margaret Clare Dewhurst
	Matthew Nicholas Dirr
	Patricia Grierson
David Greene	Carl Fredrik Valdemar Hellberg
	Si Heon Sean Hong
	Gee Woong Kim
	Taebeom Kim
	Hyun Bo Louis Kim
Alex Haw	Naoki Kotaka
	Korey Robert Kromm
	Thomas Mallory
	Jussi Taneli Mansikkamaki
	Aram Mooradian
Nicholas Puckett	Kana Moriguchi
	Kitty Caroline O'Grady
	Yuko Odaira
	Theodosia-Evdori Panagiotopoulou
	Theodora Paraschi
Nathalie Rozencwajg	Stephanie Peer
	Anna Pipilis
	Olivia Putihrai
	Katerina Scoufaridou
	Fei Fei Sophie Shan
Martina Schäfer	Eyal Shaviv
	Jaime Alberto Sol
	Natapa Sriyuksiri
	Yvonne Su Zen Tan
	Adrian Tung
	Adel Majed Zakout

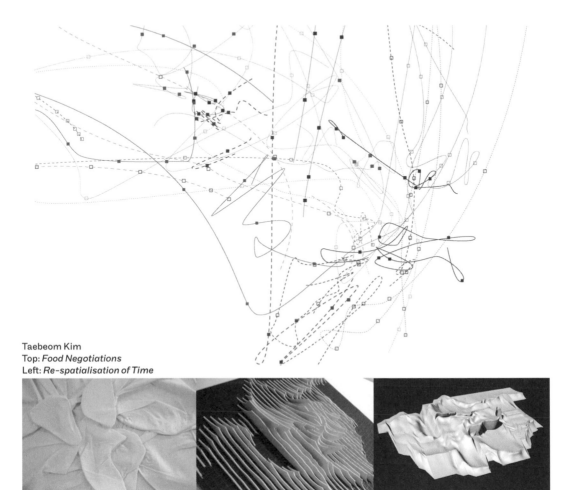

Taebeom Kim
Top: *Food Negotiations*
Left: *Re-spatialisation of Time*

Ai Bessho
Reconstruction of a Gaudí Ceiling Pattern

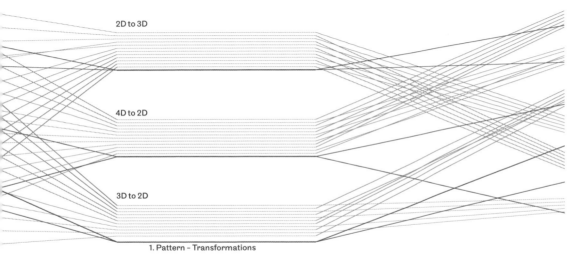

2D to 3D

4D to 2D

3D to 2D

1. Pattern - Transformations

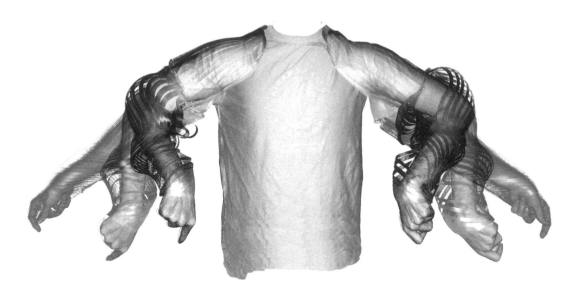

Kim Diego Azevedo
Second Skin, sleeves

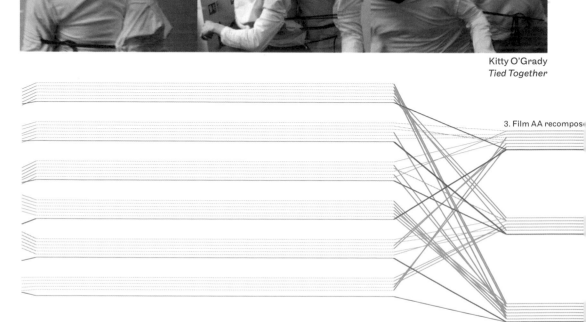

Kitty O'Grady
Tied Together

3. Film AA recompos

2. Intelligent Object

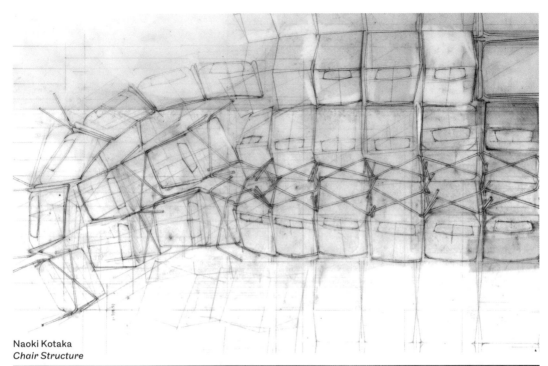

Naoki Kotaka
Chair Structure

Yuko Odaira
Rewired, phase 01

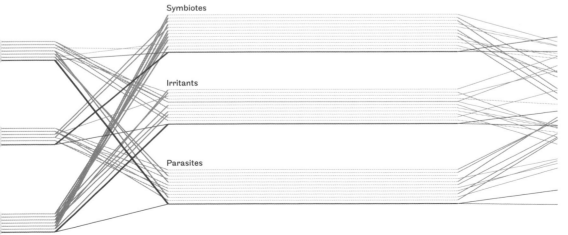

Symbiotes

Irritants

Parasites

4. Spatial Activation

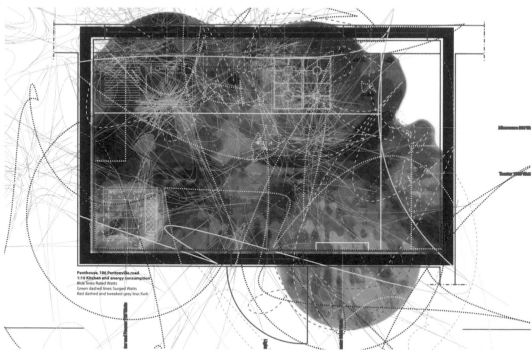

Penthouse, 186 Pentonville road.
1:10 Kitchen and energy consumption
Blue lines: Rated Watts
Green dashed lines: Surged Watts
Red dashed and tweaked grey line: Kwh

Top: Taneli Mansikkamaki
Kitchen _Energy Map

Jaime Alberto Sol
Fridge_Looking Out/Looking Down

Fei Fei Sophie Shan
Fridge_Rotations

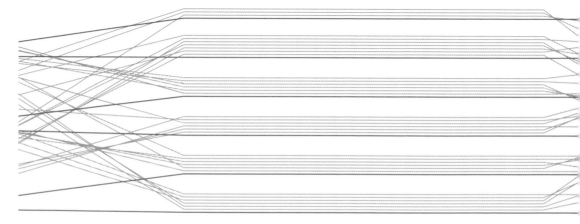

5. Draw your Fridge

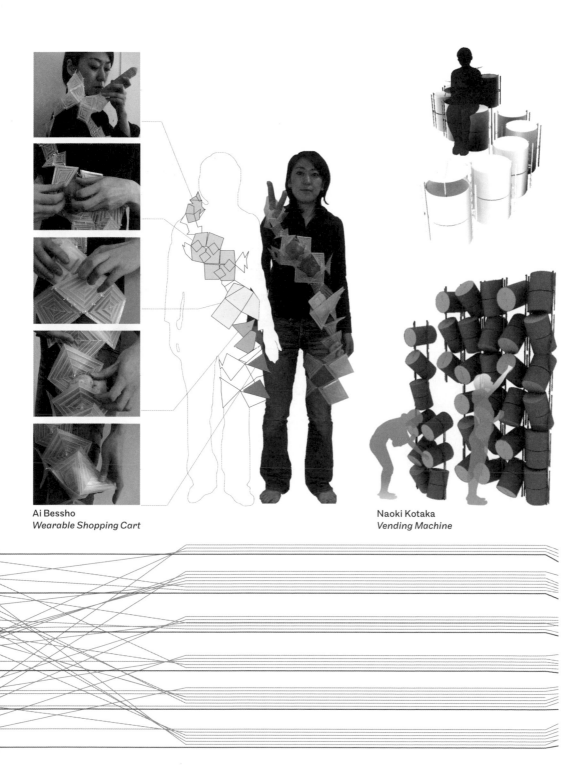

Ai Bessho
Wearable Shopping Cart

Naoki Kotaka
Vending Machine

6.1 Supermarket

THE COW

Korey Kromm
Trophies for Wedding Ceremony

Umberto Bella-Ricci / Katerina Scoufaridou
Collage for Gazebo

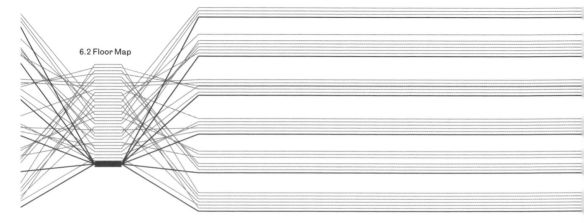

6.2 Floor Map

6.3 Supermarket

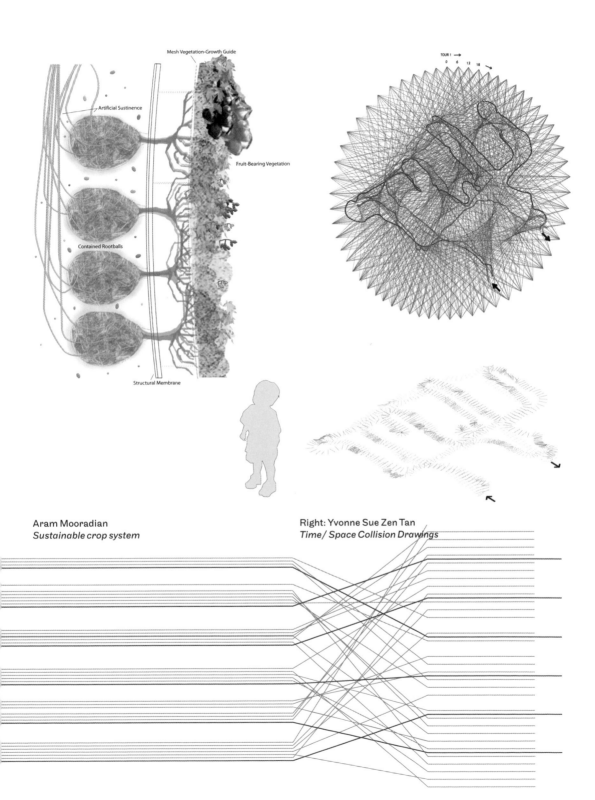

Aram Mooradian
Sustainable crop system

Right: Yvonne Sue Zen Tan
Time/ Space Collision Drawings

Installation of Intermediate Unit 3's '10 Lights'
exhibition in the Back Members' Room,
April 2006 (photo Valerie Bennett)

Intermediate School

Intermediate Unit 1

The work this year explored the physical presence of dark space. It began with the direct observation of a cow byre in an abandoned barn in France. This study ran in parallel with an exploration of Joseph Beuys's film *I Love America and America Loves Me*, in which Beuys as a shaman shares the space of a New York loft with a coyote over a three-day period. These two explorations offered very different and highly charged spatial experiences: in the cow byre, an understanding of stillness, exfoliation and dereliction as the space slowly returns to nature; in the Beuys piece an engagement with the trapped animal and the enigmatic, half-understood shamanic ritual.

Students' observations included aspects of bi-metallic corrosion, dust particles caught in the convection currents of sunlight penetrating the darkness of the barn, the absorption of light into the weathered interstitial spaces cracked by age, and the essential expediency of nature as it traces new habitats. Gathered together, these observations formed the beginnings of a sensibility with which to explore the site for the main project in Iceland.

We went to Iceland expecting the limited daylight of January and the dark magmas and black volcanic tufa of large-scale austere landscapes. We arrived in a blizzard to find a 'whiteout' in which landscape had no horizons, only differentiations of white in the phenomena of snow, cloud and steam.

Each student found a site that offered some resonance with the earlier work. Many found old industrial workings in isolated places that worked incidentally with the scale of the landscape, as industry took advantage of deep-water moorings and the abundance of thermal energy. Such industries 'squatted' these landscapes, abandoning sites as the technology moved on. Other sites were redolent of communities turning their backs on the sea to seek a life of service industries and commuting, farms no longer working and family graves undisturbed by a further generation of farm workers.

The students' building proposals offered spaces that registered such circumstances, that reordered industrial dereliction and reconnected through a self-conscious architecture the landscape and its inhabitation. Projects included a fire-testing laboratory, a hatchery for returning cod to the sea, a manuscript room on the site of the first Viking parliament, a discussion room for environmental lobbyists, a bath house for the local community, a new public cemetery, and a viewing platform to watch the Aurora Borealis.

Unit Staff: Peter Salter, Stefano Rabolli Pansera

Students: Elena Gaydar, Jiatian Gu, Sang Hoon Han, Kyoko Ito, So Jung Min, Choon Hoe Vince Ong, Spencer Owen, Kil Sue Park, Erlend Skjeseth, Hyun-Young Sung

Elena Gaydar
The Charged Space between the Coyote and the Shaman
Drawing shows a moment in time, through phenomena suggested by Beuys's film *I Love America and America Loves Me*.

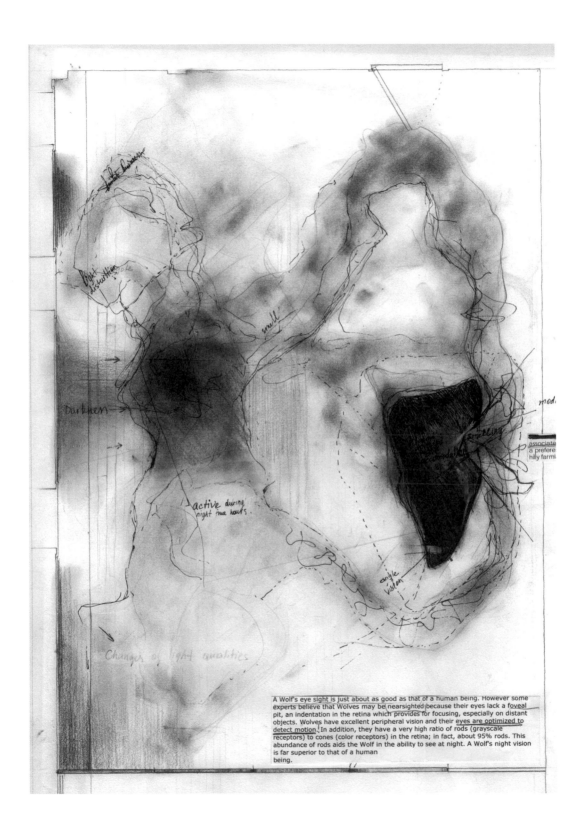

A Wolf's eye sight is just about as good as that of a human being. However some experts believe that Wolves may be nearsighted because their eyes lack a foveal pit, an indentation in the retina which provides for focusing, especially on distant objects. Wolves have excellent peripheral vision and their eyes are optimized to detect motion. In addition, they have a very high ratio of rods (grayscale receptors) to cones (color receptors) in the retina; in fact, about 95% rods. This abundance of rods aids the Wolf in the ability to see at night. A Wolf's night vision is far superior to that of a human being.

Jiatian Gu
*Platform to View the Aurora Borealis
from 'The Floating World'*
The reordering of a rusting floating dock
based on Hiroshige's woodblock prints.

Intermediate Unit 2

Inter 2 is concerned with the material stuff of the building itself. We're interested in the structural organisation of the building and its consequent architectural effect. For the last three years we have been using the 'summer pavilion' brief as the vehicle for a fairly rigorous speculative enquiry.

This year we took things one step further, and decided to build a pavilion. Not because we like 'design/build' but because we wanted to embrace the complexity of our designs not only at the level of a coordinated computer model or a rigorous technical drawing but at full scale, to address the inadequacies of drawn information first hand through construction on the shop floor.

We also wanted to test our ideas not in renderings or animations but by standing inside the space itself, through the spatial experience of space, light and material. We wanted to feel the architecture. So we decided to build.

After a research-based first term we designed and developed technical drawings of pavilions in the second term. Our selection jury included Brett Steele and Shin Egashira of the AA and architects Alison Brooks, Alex de Rijke, Allan Bell and Jamie Fobert. After a long deliberation Simon Whittle's fractal branching concept won the day.

We spent most of the third term at Hooke Park, in the timber workshop building the pavilion. Through the dedication of each individual student and the collective determination of the unit as a whole we finished and opened the pavilion on the night of Projects Review.

Unit Staff: Charles Walker, Martin Self

Students: Dana Behrman, Amandine Kastler, Tessa Katz, Eli Lui, Jesse Randzio, Evonne Tam, Hiroaki Toyoshima, Naiara Vegara, Simon Whittle, William Yam

Visiting Critics: Francis Archer, Allan Bell, Alison Brooks, Lip Chiong, Shin Egashira, Jamie Fobert, Sarah Hare, Carol Patterson, Alex de Rijke, Mark Robinson, Brett Steele

Inter 2 would like to thank our kind sponsors, without whose generous support this project would not have been possible: Finnforest UK, Maeda Corporation, Arup AGU and Architen Landrell, as well as media sponsor *Building Design*.

Opposite page, above: The Intermediate 2 team in the workshop at Hooke Park. Opposite page, below: The pavilion is made up of eight 'generations' of trefoil-shaped flanges, each scaled down by two thirds from the preceding generation.

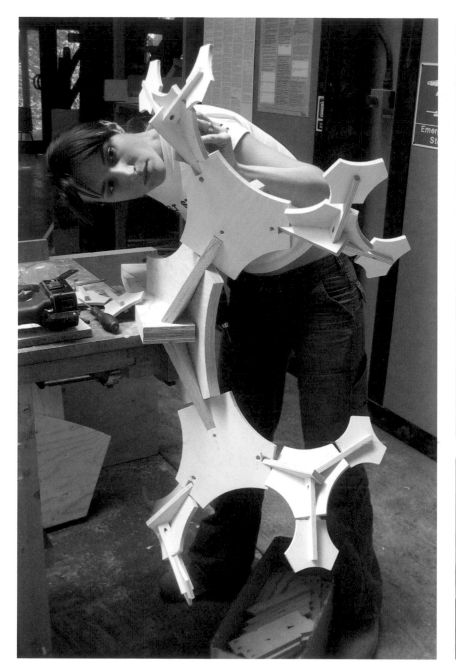

Cutting more than 2,000 components from sheets of Finnforest's Kerto laminated timber was made possible by Hooke Park's CNC cutting machine. However, the flanges and connecting beams for the largest components had to be cut and shaped by hand using circular saws.

Intermediate Unit 3

This year Inter 3 launched an experiment on two fronts. We continued our investigation into the testing, inventing and elaboration of new formal tectonics through a set of three scaled projects – Light, Room and Gallery. Students tested a range of lighting effects through these projects and, more importantly, investigated ways of shaping and controlling them through a series of formal manipulations and changing spatial conditions. The two projects by Patrick Usborne and Martin Jameson shown here rigorously evolved a set of formal principles and prototypes alongside their lighting and spatial effects, ultimately defining a symbiotic relationship between light and form.

As a parallel research we launched aainter3.net, a unit weblog, to test an online collaborative learning and teaching model. The initiative was an attempt to explore a more open platform where learning and teaching become a much more shared process within the unit – and beyond it, extending to outsiders (from the AA or elsewhere) who wish to discuss the work as it is posted. The immediate nature of the blog, whereby work is developed and viewed live, made strengths and weaknesses apparent, and invited instant criticism from unit colleagues, tutors and visitors. As such it provoked a high level of communication and dynamic learning, and made a crucial contribution to the ongoing design processes within the unit.

Unit Staff: Natasha Sandmeier, Monia De Marchi

Students: Aseel Al Yaqoub, Selina Bolton, Kevin Cash, Sandra Del Missier, Kanto Iwamura, Martin Jameson, Miho Konishi, Francesca Rogers, Patrick Usborne, MAciej Woroniecki

Workshops: International Lightscape workshop with Kazuo Iwamura of Musashi Institute of Technology, Japan, and Kaoru Mende of Lighting Detectives, LPA; Moving Postcards Workshop with Simone Muscolino, Interaction Design Lab; Graphic workshop with Zak Kyes of Zak Group

Thanks to: AA Workshop, Hitoshi Abe, Marilyn Dyer, Belinda Flaherty, Kazuo Iwamura, Zak Kyes, Antonia Loyd, Kaoru Mende, Simone Muscolino

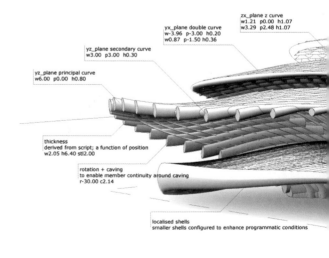

Patrick Usborne
Rooftop Gallery, Apple Store, London
Derived from an analysis of curvature, this project explores and defines
a system for filtering light into space. Through the use of scripting, a
series of shells were collectively designed. Their geometry, connectivity
and degree of permeability to light are derived through variables related
to programmatic specificity and lighting effects.

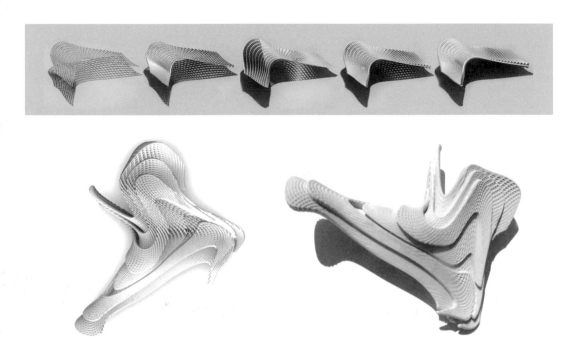

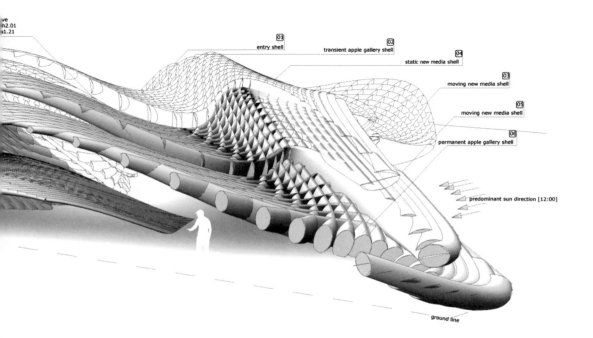

01 entry shell

02 transient apple gallery shell

04 static new media shell

03 moving new media shell

05 moving new media shell

06 permanent apple gallery shell

predominant sun direction [12:00]

ground line

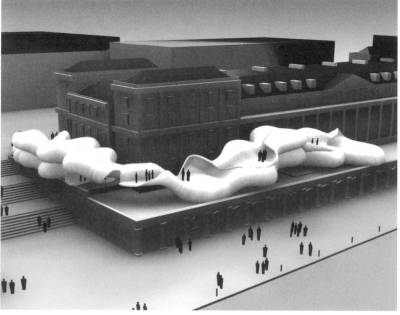

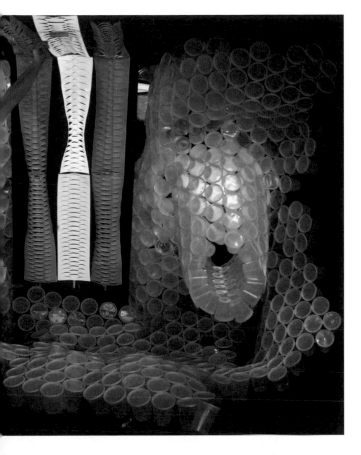

Martin Jameson
Rooftop Gallery, ICA, London
A simple modular system is used to create
a set of controls for a wide range of lighting
behaviours. This device and its modification
is packed into a hexagonal configuration and
then manipulated into a continuous surface.
The amount of natural light in each space is
controlled by altering the cone aperture and
length; light quality is controlled by the
modular cone orientation.

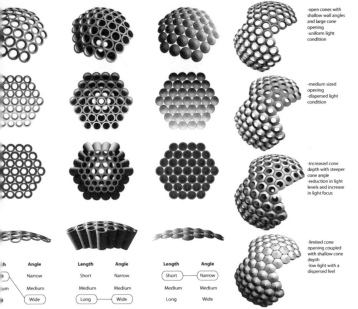

-open cones with
shallow wall angles
and large cone
opening
-uniform light
condition

-medium sized
opening
-dispersed light
condition

-increased cone
depth with steeper
cone angle
-reduction in light
levels and increase
in light focus

-limited cone
opening coupled
with shallow cone
depth
-low light with a
dispersed feel

h	Angle		Length	Angle		Length	Angle
t	Narrow		Short	Narrow		Short	Narrow
um	Medium		Medium	Medium		Medium	Medium
	Wide		Long	Wide		Long	Wide

Intermediate Unit 4

Super-High-Rise

This year Inter 4 has made an attempt to open up a discussion around the 'super-high-rise' – defined as a building more than 500 metres tall.

Over the last decade developments in hybridised structural design have made it possible to build higher than ever before. New methods of analysis and production also mean that more complex proposals can be built.

The first examples of the super-high-rise have already been built in Asia. More tall and super-tall structures are planned for Europe and the US. What could be the reasons for building so high? And how could these buildings, with their urbanistic dimensions and life-span, stimulate our cities?

Our unit has been investigating the various scales involved in the production of a super-high-rise. Students initiated a scaleless generative technique that was developed on the basis of structural, spatial and surface qualities. This technique was subsequently projected on a cube of space, making potentials visible and allowing the initial concept to be evaluated architecturally. Later, the developed concept was projected on a space of a 500-metre-high skyscraper, and developed on the basis of a specific environmental aspect.

Unit Staff: Mark Hemel, Nate Kolbe

Students: Joo Hyun Jung, Max Kahlen, Maryam Kiaie, Pil Wong Kim, Sergey Kudryashev, Chi Song Lee, Hillia Lee, Yoona Lee, Cing Geo Elida Ong, Anna Schepper, Suyeon Song

Thanks to: Jeff Turko, Gianni Botsford, Stephen Roe, Chiafang Wu, Steve Hardy, Jonas Lundberg, Peter Salter, Brett Steele, Alistair Gill, Pablo Gil, Pablo Urango-Lilo, Jan Maurits-Loecke, Djordje Stojanovic, Mike Weinstock, Chris Lee, Holger Kehne, Charles Tashima, Aristotelis Dimitrakopoulos, Ken Andrews

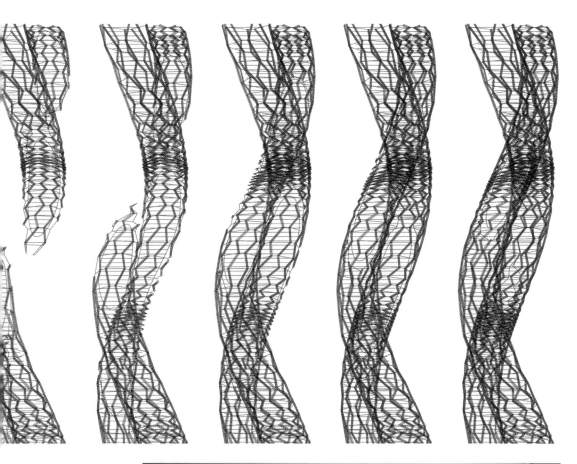

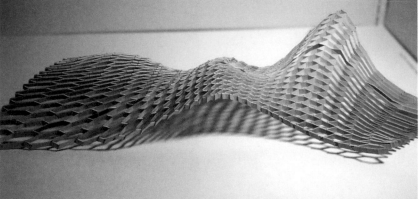

Pil Wong Kim
Helical Sun-Influenced Tower
The project is an attempt to develop an outer skin that performs as the
light-penetration control mechanism. Depth and angle of the fold lines
vary within the six-sided polygonal structure according to the local
sun-path.

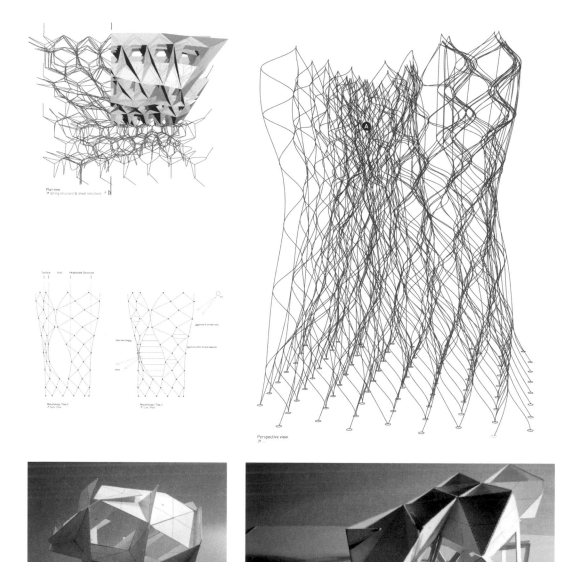

Plan view
↗ Sitting structure & sheet structure   A

Surface   Void   Inhabitable Structure

Morphology / Seq 1
↗ Side View

Morphology / Seq 2
↗ Line View

Perspective view
↗

Max Kahlen
Skyscraper Without Floors
In concept the project is a 'crystallised mass' of stability walls,
attempting to free up the skyscraper from a regular positioning
of floors.

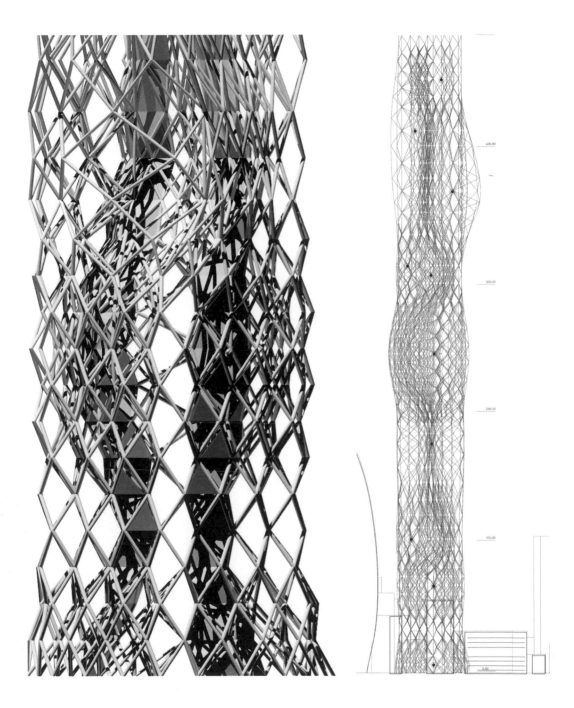

Intermediate Unit 6

Architectural Still-Life:
Vast Public Space

This year Inter 6 had two main themes: a notion of the 'digital sketch', and new formations of public space.

Three short projects from the first term guided the main project. These were a workshop on the potential of algorithms; a questioning of the limitations of 'simulation' as part of a design process, and experimentations into diagramming 'what is a situation'.

Mechanisms of sketching form and space in the computer served as a starting point to question what can be meant by public space. Each student developed their own idea of what it means to sketch into 'custom-designed digital interfaces'.

New ideas of structure and tectonics generated within the sketch interface served as the basis for the main project, the creation of 'vast public space'. Starting from real examples of truly huge spaces, the brief called for new

ideas of 'relationship', to take new account of spaces of encounter and their formation.

Throughout the year we hosted a series of workshops: Theory, 3d/4d Modelling, Animation, Scripting, Web Design, Interface Design and Gaming.

Unit Staff: Alistair Gill, Veronika Schmid

Students: Erlend Bakke-Eidsaa, Wai Tong Thomas Chan, Sea Eun Cho, Royia Forouhar Abadeh, Fedor Gridnev, Rebecca Harral, Yo Murata, Derin Ozken, Jorgen Tandberg, Piotr Topinkski

The unit would like to give special thanks to Daniel Bosia, Mark Cousins, Oliver Domeisen, Christiane Fashek, Nate Kolbe, George L Legendre, Paula Pelosi, Brett Steele, Prof Alex Scott, Tristan Simmonds, Frank Stella, Moe Suksudpaisarn, Prof Alberto Toscano, Bernard Vere, Bob van Winkle

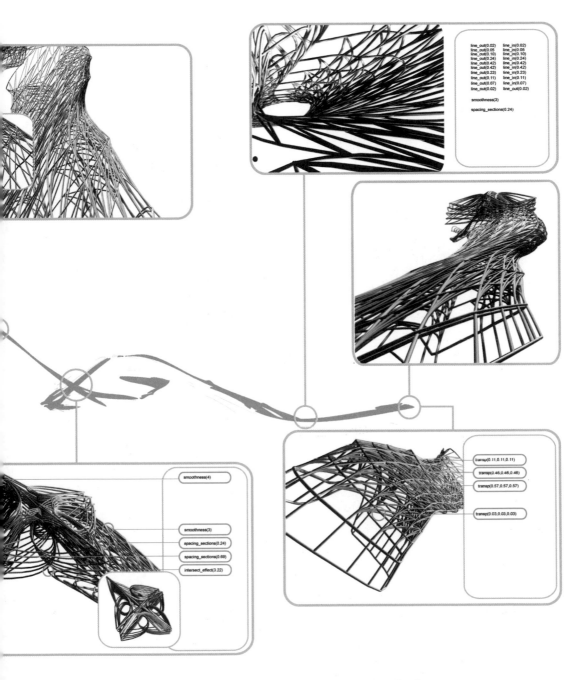

line_out(0.02)   line_in(0.02)
line_out(0.05)   line_in(0.05)
line_out(0.10)   line_in(0.10)
line_out(0.24)   line_in(0.24)
line_out(0.42)   line_in(0.42)
line_out(0.42)   line_in(0.42)
line_out(0.23)   line_in(0.23)
line_out(0.11)   line_in(0.11)
line_out(0.07)   line_in(0.07)
line_out(0.02)   line_out(0.02)

smoothness(3)

spacing_sections(0.24)

smoothness(4)

smoothness(3)
spacing_sections(0.24)
spacing_sections(0.69)
intersect_effect(3.22)

transp(0.11,0.11,0.11)
transp(0.46,0.46,0.46)
transp(0.57,0.57,0.57)
transp(0.03,0.03,0.03)

Jorgen Tandberg
Painted Space
Above and far left: Explorations into painterly
lines as generative logic to new formations of
public space at Oslo Central Station.

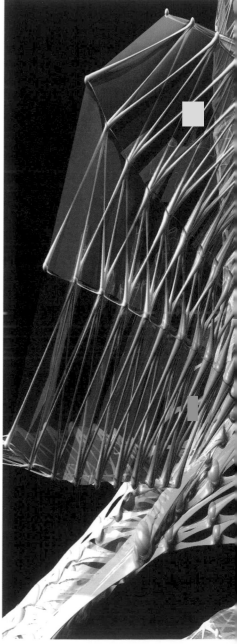

Thomas Chan
Hyde Park: New Public Event Space
Left and below: Detail of tectonic system.
Far right: Interactive custom–designed digital
interface; sketch as the creation of tectonics.

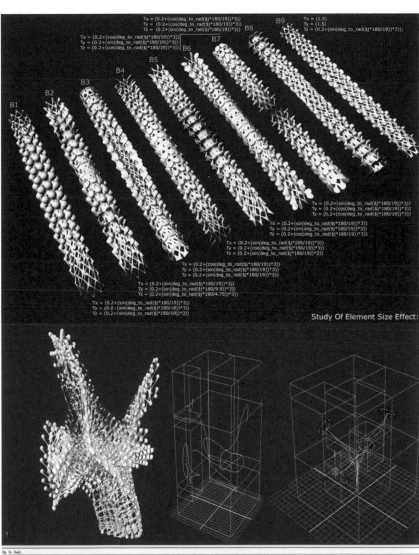

Intermediate Unit 7

Inter 7's projects, which range in scale from the national, to the urban, to the detail, share a single preoccupation: to expose the link between mental health and space.

Stephanie Edwards (Second Year)
Reconfiguring St Clement's Hospital
This project (shown overleaf) defines the conditions for the staff and patients who live and work in St Clement's Hospital, a former workhouse or 'prison by a milder name'. It explores whether the 1849-era hierarchy extends throughout the hospital today. At the outset, the operational and behavioural aspects on one particular ward were analysed. The intended timetable initiated by the staff was compared with the actual timetable followed by the patients. This displayed the many physical and non-physical restrictions within the ward and its constant fluctuation throughout the day. The initial study probed efforts to flatten the hierarchy, for example through the removal of a formal uniform, and challenged the system within the ward as well as the relationships between staff, patient and visitor. In response to the insight gained, architectural, organisational and urban propositions were made. The process from admission to discharge was scrutinised and redirected to facilitate speedy recovery.
The services located at St Clement's are gradually being moved to purpose-built sites. As areas are abandoned, an urban proposal aims to integrate the community through shared use.

Freda Yuen (Third Year)
Preventing Conflict
An investigation of how to prevent conflict in mental health wards, the project works at three different scales:
Component Analysis of anti-ligature products within a ward revealed their unintended influence on patient behaviour. All subsequent design proposals were tested against anti-ligature criteria.

Architecture Repetition of components in existing ward environments amplifies their effect upon the movement of service users, exaggerates hierarchies between patients and staff and increases tension, leading to self-harm and violent conflict: this was reversed.
Policy The ward manager plays a central role in the definition of the ward environment and has an intimate understanding of patients' needs. Adamization was proposed as a policy that optimises and cements this key relationship.

Unit Masters: Markus Miessen, Matthew Murphy

Students: Viola Carnelutti, Stephanie Edwards, Caroline Fansa, Jin Kim, Angela Lim, Theo Petrides, Nikhil Raj, Talya Sandbank, Shintaro Tsuruoka, Freda Yuen

ADAMIZATION
CAMPAIGN

Estates and Facilities Management > Policy and Guidance > Built Environment > Actions> Ideas

Condition 2 : Increase Hierarchy within Patients to Encourage Cooperation

Uniformity of space is used to calm patients who have higher chances for deliberate self-harm. Uncooperative patients will be deprived from personalizing their space. This system also promotes good conduct through understanding patients' rights to freedom.

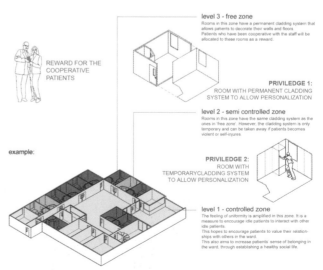

REWARD FOR THE COOPERATIVE PATIENTS

example:

level 3 - free zone
Rooms in this zone have a permanent cladding system that allows patients to decorate their walls and floors. Patients who have been cooperative with the staff will be allocated to these rooms as a reward.

PRIVILEDGE 1:
ROOM WITH PERMANENT CLADDING SYSTEM TO ALLOW PERSONALIZATION

level 2 - semi controlled zone
Rooms in this zone have the same cladding system as the ones in 'free zone'. However, the cladding system is only temporary and can be taken away if patients becomes violent or self-injures.

PRIVILEDGE 2:
ROOM WITH TEMPORARYCLADDING SYSTEM TO ALLOW PERSONALIZATION

level 1 - controlled zone
The feeling of uniformity is amplified in this zone. It is a measure to encourage idle patients to interact with other idle patients.
This hopes to encourage patients to value their relationships with others in the ward.
This also aims to increase patients' sense of belonging in the ward, through establishing a healthy social life.

source: Mornington Unit, St. Pancras Hospital

Design Specifications within a Mental Health Ward

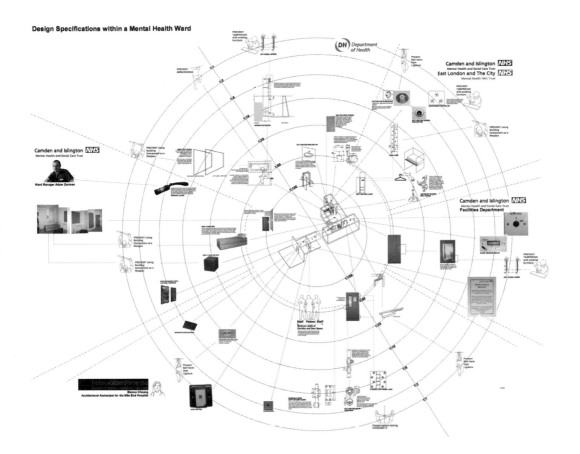

Stephanie Edwards
Reconfiguring St Clement's Hospital

Unfolded time based plans analysing patient and staff timetables

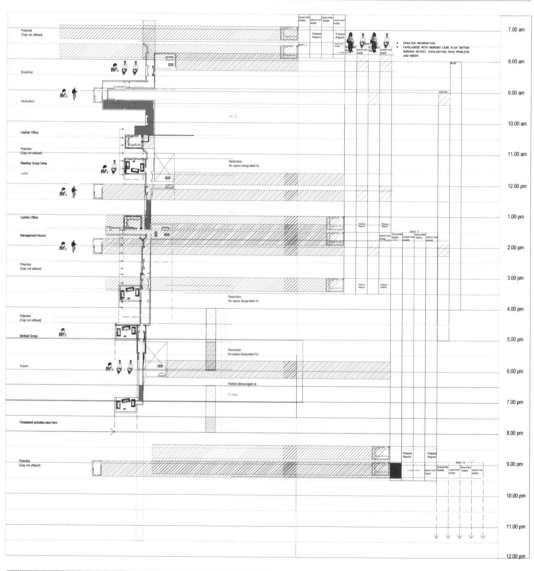

St. Clements Hospital

Location Map
Building(s) of interest

Potential gaps for interventions

Compulsory activities

Gaps between timetabled activities

Patients cannot access

Visitors intervention

Patient Report   write a report of allocated patient's

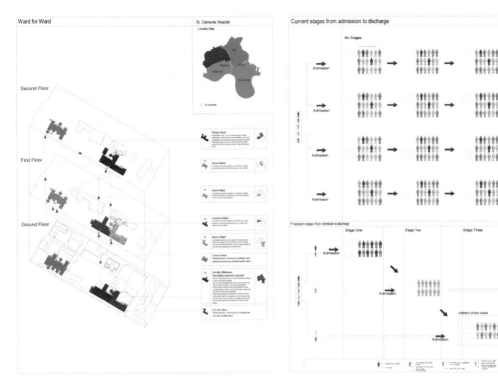

Ward for Ward

St Clements Hospital
Location Map

Second Floor

First Floor

Ground Floor

Current stages from admission to discharge

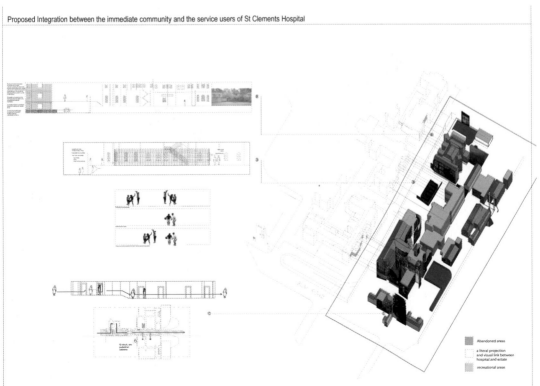

Proposed Integration between the immediate community and the service users of St Clements Hospital

Abandoned areas

a literal projection and visual link between hospital and estate

recreational areas

Intermediate Unit 8

The students began the year investigating techniques of organising component-based aggregations as a catalyst for the production of forms and structures which are parametrically controlled by manipulating local connections, so as to generate precise global formations. They designed a repetitive interlocking system as a three-dimensional mesh, differentially distributed to create a garment specifically tailored to fit their own body. In addition to the physical models, scripting exercises were pursued that highlighted the systematic exploration of the projects through 3d modelling tools.

The brief for the main design project undertaken in terms 2 and 3 was to develop proposals for a mixed-use, mid-size building located in the fashion district of Omotesando in Tokyo. The students started the project by developing spatial organisations through the analysis of ruled surfaces. From this analysis they each developed their own detailed programmatic and organisational models which addressed the requirements of circulation, activities and spatial effects.

Unit Staff: Yusuke Obuchi, Eugene Han

Students: Christopher Johan Dyvik, Sunny Zhou Bin He, Jin Hong Jeon, Hyun Bae Jun, Kang Joon Lee, Bolam Lee, Anna Nagel, Maryam Pousti, Sakiko Watanabe, Jung Joon Yun

Visiting Critics: Javier Castanon, Alan Dempsey, Shin Egashira, Alistair Gill, Steven Hardy, Sam Jacoby, Holger Kehne, Simon Kim, George L Legendre, Jonas Lundberg, Stephen Roe, Anne Save de Beaurecueil, Martina Schäfer, Martin Self, Brett Steele, Vasilis Stroumpakos, Charles Tashima, Tom Verebes, Jinbok Wee, Chiafang Wu

Thanks to Marilyn Dyer, Belinda Flaherty, Antonia Loyd, Joel Newman

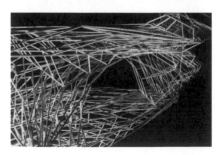

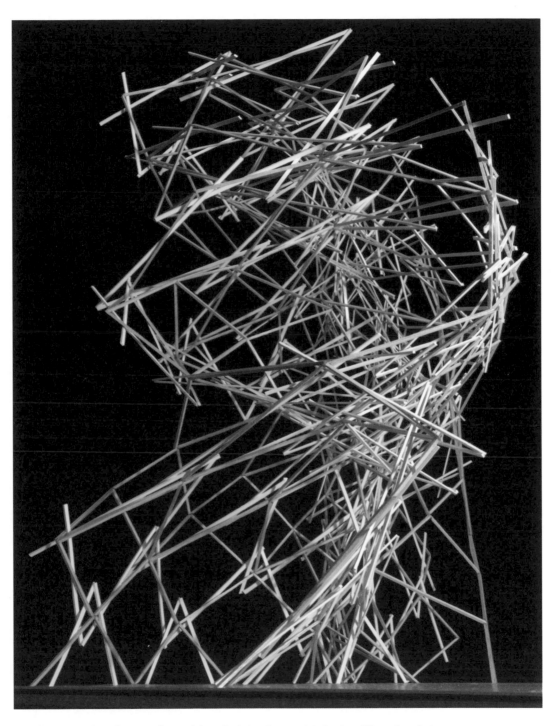

Left: Component-based aggregation models and ruled surface models developed through analogue and digital production processes (Bolam Lee).
Above: Based on the interlocking double ruled surfaces, structural systems were organised according to structural rigidity and programmatic distribution (Christopher Dyvik).

```
proc procMobiusBandBase()
{
        float $xScale=`floatSliderGrp -q -v fsgXscale`;
        float $zScale=`floatSliderGrp -q -v fsgZscale`;
        int $i;
        for($i=0; $i<101; $i++)
        {
                float $rotateAngle=(float)3.6*$i;
                float $rotateAngleRad=`deg_to_rad $rotateAngle`;
                float $moveX=$xScale*cos($rotateAngleRad);
                float $moveZ=$zScale*sin($rotateAngleRad);
                curve -d 1 -p 0 -1 0 -p 0 1 0 -k 0 -k 1 ;
                move $moveX 0 $moveZ;
                rotate -r 0 (-$rotateAngle) 0;
        }
}

proc procMobiusBand()
{
        select curve1 curve2 curve3 curve4 curve5 curve6 curve7 curve8 curve9 curve10
                curve11 curve12 curve13 curve14 curve15 curve16 curve17 curve18 curve19
curve20
                curve21 curve22 curve23 curve24 curve25 curve26 curve27 curve28 curve29
curve30
                curve31 curve32 curve33 curve34 curve35 curve36 curve37 curve38 curve39
curve40
                curve41 curve42 curve43 curve44 curve45 curve46 curve47 curve48 curve49
curve50
                curve51 curve52 curve53 curve54 curve55 curve56 curve57 curve58 curve59
curve60
                curve61 curve62 curve63 curve64 curve65 curve66 curve67 curve68 curve69
curve70
                curve71 curve72 curve73 curve74 curve75 curve76 curve77 curve78 curve79
curve80
                curve81 curve82 curve83 curve84 curve85 curve86 curve87 curve88 curve89
curve90
                curve91 curve92 curve93 curve94 curve95 curve96 curve97 curve98 curve99
curve100 curve101;
        string $wire[]=`ls -sl`;
        int $totalWire=`size($wire)`;
        int $i;
        for($i=0; $i<$totalWire; $i++)
        {
                if($i!=0)
                {
                        float $angle=(float)180/100*$i;
                        select -cl;
                        select -tgl $wire[$i];
                        rotate -r 0 0 $angle;
                }
        }
}

proc procRenderMobius()
{
        select curve1 curve2 curve3 curve4 curve5 curve6 curve7 curve8 curve9 curve10
                curve11 curve12 curve13 curve14 curve15 curve16 curve17 curve18 curve19
```

```
curve20
                curve21 curve22 curve23 curve24 cu
                curve31 curve32 curve33 curve34 cu
                curve41 curve42 curve43 curve44 cu
                curve51 curve52 curve53 curve54 cu
                curve61 curve62 curve63 curve64 cu
                curve71 curve72 curve73 curve74 cu
                curve81 curve82 curve83 curve84 cu
                curve91 curve92 curve93 curve94 cu
curve101;

                loft -ar 0;

}

proc procCircles()
{
        float $xScale=`floatSliderGrp -q -v fsgXscale1`;
        float $zScale=`floatSliderGrp -q -v fsgZscale1`;

        for($i=0; $i<101; $i++)
        {
                float $rotateAngle=(float)3.6*$i;
                float $rotateAngleRad=`deg_to_rad $rotateAng
                float $moveX=$xScale*cos($rotateAngleRad);
                float $moveZ=$zScale*sin($rotateAngleRad);
                circle -c 0 0 0 -nr 0 0 1 -sw 36 -r 1 -d 3 -ut 0 -
                move $moveX 0 $moveZ;
                rotate -r 0 (-$rotateAngle) 0;
        }
}

proc procRotationCircle()
{
        int $numberOfRotation =`intSliderGrp -q -v isgNumRotat
        if(`checkBox -q -v cbXaxisCircle`)

        select nurbsCircle1 nurbsCircle2 nurbsCircle3 nurbsCircle
nurbsCircle8 nurbsCircle9 nurbsCircle10
                        nurbsCircle11 nurbsCircle12 nurbsCir
nurbsCircle17 nurbsCircle18 nurbsCircle19 nurbsCircle20
                        nurbsCircle21 nurbsCircle22 nurbsCir
nurbsCircle27 nurbsCircle28 nurbsCircle29 nurbsCircle30
                        nurbsCircle31 nurbsCircle32 nurbsCir
nurbsCircle37 nurbsCircle38 nurbsCircle39 nurbsCircle40
                        nurbsCircle41 nurbsCircle42 nurbsCir
nurbsCircle47 nurbsCircle48 nurbsCircle49 nurbsCircle50
                        nurbsCircle51 nurbsCircle52 nurbsCir
nurbsCircle57 nurbsCircle58 nurbsCircle59 nurbsCircle60
                        nurbsCircle61 nurbsCircle62 nurbsCir
nurbsCircle67 nurbsCircle68 nurbsCircle69 nurbsCircle70
                        nurbsCircle71 nurbsCircle72 nurbsCir
nurbsCircle77 nurbsCircle78 nurbsCircle79 nurbsCircle80
                        nurbsCircle81 nurbsCircle82 nurbsCir
nurbsCircle87 nurbsCircle88 nurbsCircle89 nurbsCircle90
                        nurbsCircle91 nurbsCircle92 nurbsCir
nurbsCircle97 nurbsCircle98 nurbsCircle99 nurbsCircle100 nurbsCir
```

rve27 curve28 curve29 curve30
rve37 curve38 curve39 curve40
rve47 curve48 curve49 curve50
rve57 curve58 curve59 curve60
rve67 curve68 curve69 curve70
rve77 curve78 curve79 curve80
rve87 curve88 curve89 curve90
rve97 curve98 curve99 curve100

1;

urbsCircle6 nurbsCircle7

e14 nurbsCircle15 nurbsCircle16

e24 nurbsCircle25 nurbsCircle26

e34 nurbsCircle35 nurbsCircle36

e44 nurbsCircle45 nurbsCircle46

e54 nurbsCircle55 nurbsCircle56

e64 nurbsCircle65 nurbsCircle66

e74 nurbsCircle75 nurbsCircle76

e84 nurbsCircle85 nurbsCircle86

e94 nurbsCircle95 nurbsCircle96

Sakiko Watanabe created Mel script to parametrically control the geometrical relation of 100 circles to form a continuous spatial envelope. Gradient surface organisations were developed with the same script to highlight the programmatic differentiations.

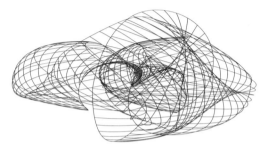

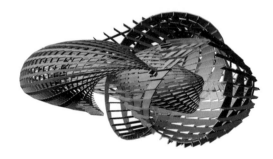

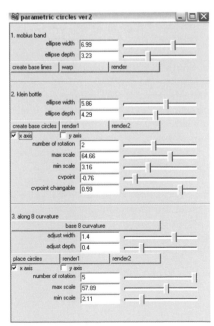

Intermediate Unit 9

Lost on Re-make Island

Just how many films, TV programmes and songs are re-makes these days? Lots. The phenomenon is nothing new: 'Renaissance' literally means 're-birth'. Anyone who copies original paintings and distributes them into an economy claiming their re-makes are 'The Real Thing' is a forger. Inter 9's first-term project taught students how to become architectural forgers. Having adopted the guise of an iconic twentieth-century architect, each student re-made an iconic project by a fellow Starchitect, *but in their own style*. In the process, questions about signature style and content were unfolded in a kind of role-play surrendering one's own 'authentic' authorial presence.

Akis Pattihis became Mies van der Rohe becoming Archigram. That is to say, Archigram's seminal *Walking Cities* vision was re-made from the point of view of Mies's austere rational planning rubric. The result was a beached version of Archigram's itinerant city on the move.

The study of re-makes set the scene for the main project: the phantasmagoric site of real life re-makes and forgeries, Dubai. There, in true Baudrillard-style, the copy has to outperform the original in every sense, putting into question the primary function of the architect as form-giver or form-recycler. Students each developed proposals for new islands off the new artificial coastline (was 45 km long, will be 1,500 km long by 2025).

Inspired by Romantic paintings of the eighteenth century, Claude Ballini's vision for Dubai, The Mountain, turns the city of Dubai into a sublime spectacle of feverish hubris. Made of Dubai's demolished buildings, The Mountain is an absurd escapist retreat that out-'reals' the 'real' of Dubai.

Unit Masters: Shumon Basar, Oliver Domeisen

Students: Claude Ballini, Kyuho Choi, Erandi de Silva, Damien Figueras, Rika Horiki, Kin Wai Kevin Hung, Soo Hyun Jin, Jin Ho Park, Akis Pattihis, Jae Won Yi, Hong Chieh Yow

Critics: Elio Caccavale, Frances Mikuriya, Alistair Gill, Natasha Sandmeier, Sam Jacoby, Cathy Hawley, Rubens Azevedo, Francesca Hughes, Anne Save de Beaurecueil, Madelon Vriesendorp, Marina Lathouri, Roberto Bogazzo, Aristede Antonas, Kathy Battista, Pascal Schöning, Martina Schäfer, Jay Merrick, Henrik Rothe, Monia De Marchi

Thanks to Antonia Carver, Marilyn Dyer, Ben Fisher at Nakheel, Belinda Flaherty, Antonia Loyd, George Katodrytis, Joel Newman, Madelon Vriesendorp, Brett Steele, Tariq K. Zayyat

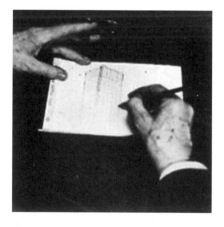

Claude Ballini
The Mountain
Above: Gazing upon Dubai from the vantage point of a twenty-first-century Romantic traveller.
The climb to the top of the island reveals a modern sublime.
Left: Mies van der Rohe's genius hands at work.

Claude Ballini
Above: *The Mountain* seen from Dubai beach
Right: An escalator leads visitors to viewing apexes

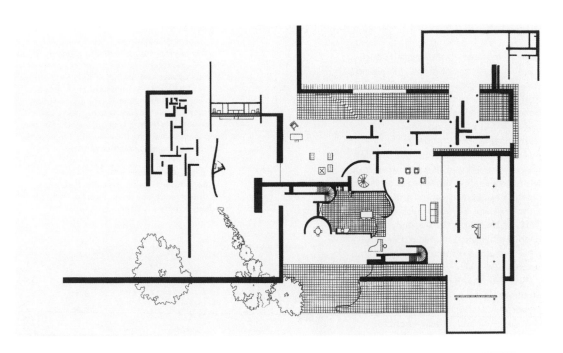

Akis Pattihis
Top: A 'sampler of Mies's greatest works' conflated into a single plan
Above: *Mies's Walking City in Chicago*

Intermediate Unit 10

Inter 10 mapped various aspects of the King's Cross development site using a range of methods of interaction with its inhabitants and visitors, their social behaviour and their routines of urban life until specific issues emerged.

Employing the 1:1 model as intervention, we are examining in real terms the ways in which we can engage simultaneously with the realities of the existing built environment and the culture or way of life of its residents. This, we believe, is the territory where architecture and urbanism meet and where we can examine the relationship between the two.

By working with the residents and challenging them to engage with our structures we hope to produce results that surprise and inform – both the participants and ourselves. It is this live interaction between the work and the community which sets our agenda and drives the process onwards. We use the model to establish a forum for ourselves in which to make profound observations and learn from the ground up how our work impacts on an existing community.

We work on a human scale, but not because we are concerned only with the small scale. The small scale allows us to uncover issues that are relevant across a wide range of scales. The proposals of the unit address these different scales referring back to the knowledge gained through the direct interaction.

Unit Staff: Andreas Lang, Kathrin Böhm

Students: Badintra Balankura, Amelia Blair, Joo Yun Cho, Bonnie L Y Chu, Tamao Hashimoto, Hiromichi Hata, Jenny Kagan, Dajung Kim, Yong Bum Kim, Marilia Spanou

External Students: Lena Tutunjian, Jenny-Elisa Schäffer, Bianca Thelmo

Bonnie L Y Chu
Plague of Occupation
After working intensively with young people at the Copenhagen Youth Project, the proposal is to set up an autonomous youth organisation. The aim of this organisation is to create a tower, a headquarters for the organisation which empowers youths to express themselves freely through occupying other public spaces, subverting the rules and limitations currently imposed on them and their surroundings.

Control is reciprocal – access over things others want is essential for control. Control cannot be eliminated but it can be used in mutually beneficial ways.

.

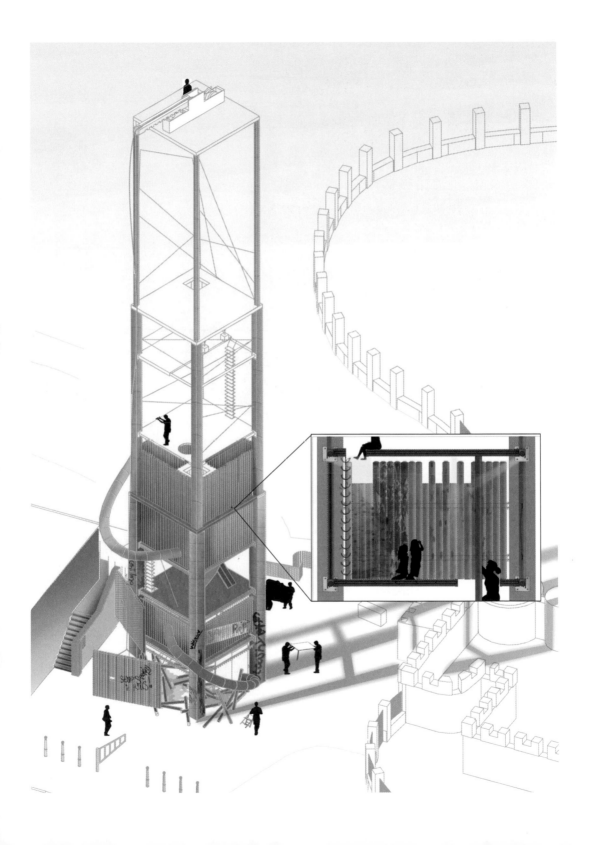

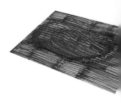

Plane Space.

1. Push the button to unlock the model and start to raise up it.   2. Pull back the model.   3. Keep on pulling back the model.

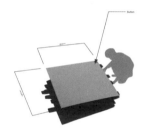

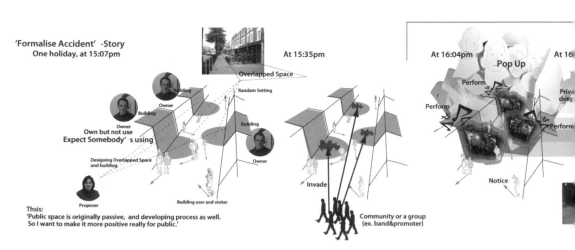

'Formalise Accident' -Story
One holiday, at 15:07pm

At 15:35pm

At 16:04pm   At 16

Overlapped Space

Pop Up

Building

Owner

Randam Setting

Perform   Priva
deep

Owner

Building

Perform   Perform

Own but not use
Expect Somebody' s using

Designing Overlapped Space
and building.

Owner

Notice

Invade

Proposer   Building user and visiter

Community or a group
(ex. band&promoter)

Thsis:
'Public space is originally passive, and developing process as well.
So I want to make it more positive really for public.'

Hiromichi Hata
Formalised Accidents
The initial research focused on negotiating the territorial status of
spaces along Caledonian Road which seem to belong to the public
pavement but are owned and controlled by the local shops. The project
involved hosting a series of spontaneous and non-commercial events
that allowed different user groups to temporarily claim the space.
The initial tests on site helped to establish the concept of a 'formalised

Building has designed.

Space is getting more volume.

Space rises up taking volume.

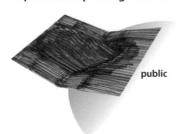

public

public

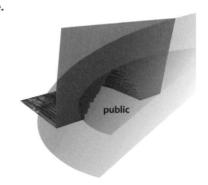

public

4. Raise up the extended model.

5. Raise up the model up to when it stands completely.

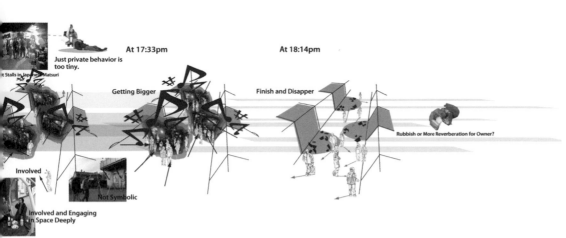

At 17:33pm

Just private behavior is too tiny.

t Stalls in Japanese Matsuri

Getting Bigger

At 18:14pm

Finish and Disapper

Rubbish or More Reverberation for Owner?

Involved

Not Symbolic

Involved and Engaging in Space Deeply

accident'. The final proposition takes as its site of speculation the central boulevard of the proposed King's Cross development. A network of 'pop-up' structures will add an important layer of spontaneity to the street. The 'pop-ups' will allow for a wide range of temporary activities on different scales to take place and help to set up new and unexpected relationships.

'AA Diploma Honours Students 2004/05'
exhibition opening, October 2005
(photo Chris Fenn)

Diploma School

Diploma Unit 1

Adaptation: The History of Things

Diploma Unit 1 approaches architecture via the modification and adjustment of the already existing. Re-use, recombination and re-contextualisation of things found are means by which we can define architectural design invention. Within a systems-based approach, we explore the possibilities of designing out of the history of things via the adaptation and augmentation of found materials, structures, processes, sites and uses. Such products are adjusted and augmented within a strategy of iterative, emergent design permutations and evolutions. Material is placed within alternative contexts and technologies often using contemporary understandings of low-tech materialisations.

The projects selected here offer two approaches. Both operate within a sensitive understanding of the landscape and its associated scalar, environmental and cultural values. The first project emerges out of the analysis of various forms of traditional timber constructions including stave churches, bridges and large span timber structures. These methods are re-mastered within lamination technologies while pushing the envelope of timber on a large scale. The second project takes a post-industrial landscape (slate quarry) and seeks to redirect its history into an alternative future through, among other things, short rotation coppice to generate power as a biomass fuel. In both projects, the scale of the material is set against the scale of the landscape in equal measure.

As in all years, each student is asked to devise and develop their own comprehensive design thesis within the framework of the unit. This method is process-based, whereby the work develops through stages of refinement with numerous feedback loops and layers that include material strategies, sites and programmes.

Unit Staff: Charles Tashima, Tyen Masten

Students: Teresa Cheung, Farah Ghanim, Sarah Entwistle, Gidon Fuehrer, Robert Gluckman, Panayiotis Hadjichristofis, Mellis Haward, Ruth Kedar, Takamasa Kikuchi, James McDermott, Andrew McMullan, Catherine Pease, Nicholas Pozner, Thomas Smith, Chih-Wei (David) Weng

y UP 01/1

y LP 01
y LP 02
y LP 03
y LP 04

y Members Parting:

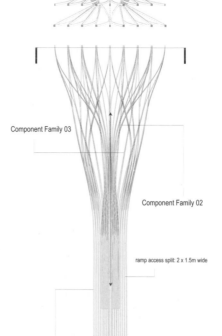

Component Family 03

Component Family 02

ramp access split: 2 x 1.5m wide

Component Family 01

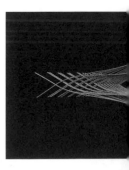

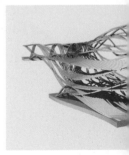

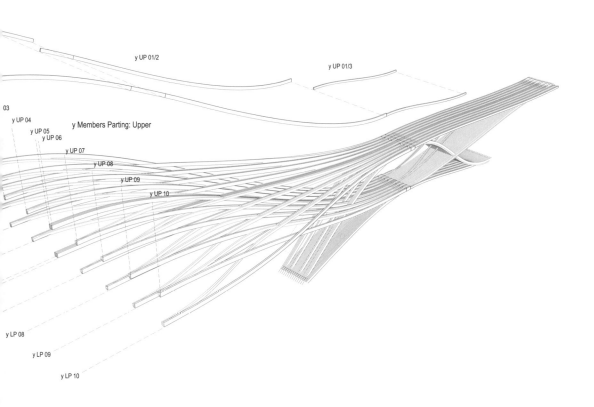

y UP 01/2

y UP 01/3

03

y UP 04

y Members Parting: Upper

y UP 05
y UP 06

y UP 07

y UP 08

y UP 09

y UP 10

y LP 08

y LP 09

y LP 10

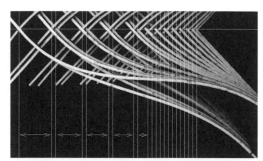

Tom Smith
A system of laminated timber integrating large-span spaces into the landscape: Waverley Valley, Edinburgh
The thesis aims to demonstrate a systematic deployment of large-span spaces integrated into the landscape. The production technology of re-engineered timber allows for mass-customisation of parts according to a wide range of geometry. An assembly logic determining component scale evolves from the production technology within the parameters set by restricted site access. Edinburgh city centre is introduced as a test site for the system.

Top: Constituent parts of bifurcated large-span space.
Far left: Plan and section of nested access routes.
Left, below: Single-bay section model investigating varied porosity between internal and sheltered external spaces; log bridge case study located in Siberia.

Sarah Entwistle
Defining infrastrucutres of slate waste
Topography: Ffestiniog Quarry, North Wales
The project aims to position itself within the
lineage of landscape theory, through an
understanding of contemporary attitudes
towards post-industrial landscapes as
comparable to the nineteenth-century
perception of ancient ruins set against
verdant Italian hills. Sites such as the Welsh
quarry pits are becoming places of pilgrimage
infused with romantic notions of our
industrial past, to be revered and emulated. It
is this sentimental and distorted perception of
such sites that the project aims to address.

The disused quarries of North Wales create
a parallel topography to the rugged mountain
terrain which they have been dug out of. Seen
from above, it is hard to discern whether they
are geological formations or manmade. The
forms that have been generated from a
seemingly random process of extraction and
tipping are simultaneously organic and highly
structured.

Top: Ground remediation section through a
slice of terrace waste tip illustrating the
resultant surface conditions.
Centre: Typical landscape fragment showing
willow growing beds, hiking paths, bat roosts,
camping and thermal pools.
Bottom, from left to right: Masterplan phasing
2000, 2007, 2012, 2016, 2024, starting from
the final years of quarry extraction to the
development of waste-tip terraces, ground
remediation, and hiking trails; layering
sequence using compaction of graded waste
and CIPS grouting to generate cavity wall
structures; typical quarry showing circulation
networks of circular haulage routes, track
mounted buckets, and waste slate against
natural dip or rockface.

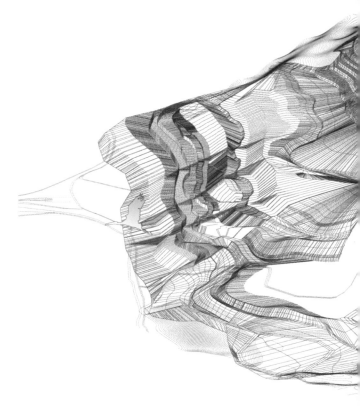

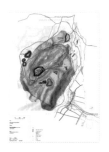
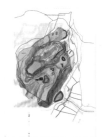

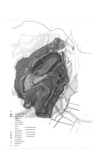

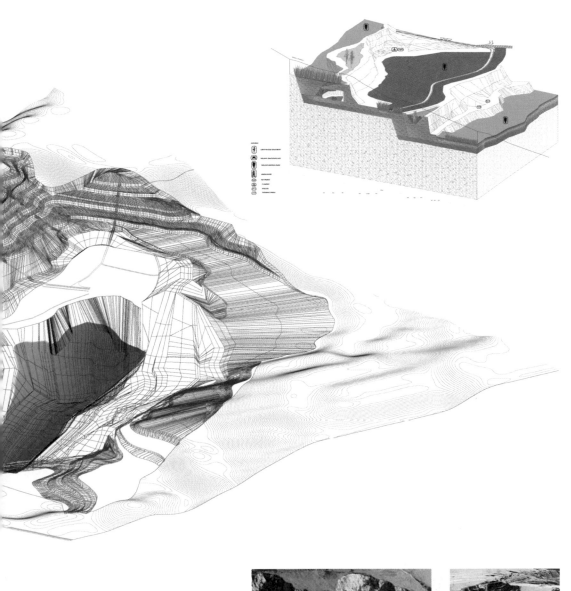

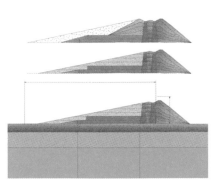

Diploma Unit 2

Liquid Urbanism
The unit worked on developing intricate formal organisations to cultivate a flexible and multi-scalar diffusion of different sources of energy in both architectural and urban environments for the creation of a new Social Service of Commerce (SESC) Centre along the border between Paraísopolis favela and the affluent Morumbi neighbourhood in Sao Paulo, Brazil. Environmental mediation systems were developed to promote different types of cultural–environmental event structures by conditioning and creating a variety of different ambient effects, so as to pro-duce a fusion of structure, form and flow.

The ultimate goal was to promote a more symbiotic relationship between culture, environmental conditioning and the natural landscape, mediating between macro climates and micro climates, as well as between formal and informal socio-economic and cultural entities. To activate an effective dissipation of energy transfers, the unit focused on proliferating micro-scale environmental mediation devices that transform and mutate according to (and eventually intricately relate) a multi-plicity of different-scaled macro-force systems, enabling new flows of energy in areas where currently none exist.

Students worked on achieving a cultural and environmental inter-modality by creating varied field condition meshworks with the computational techniques of variable subdivision tessellation and recursive primitive proliferation. Subdivision is an algorithmic computational modelling tool that responds to variable topological and structural forces by generating a system of successively refined polyhedral organisations. Like blood capillaries, its efficacy in its proliferation is obtained through a miniaturisation and multiplication of channels to create an intelligent network of branching vectors.

Unit Staff: Anne Save de Beaurecueil, Franklin Lee

Students: Juan Carlo Calma, Yun Hee Choi, Graig Delany, Celia Imaz, Ricky Rui Li, Jee Seon Lim, Rudo Manokore, Hayssam Moubayed, Inés Primo de Rivera, Phivos Skroumbelos

Consultants: Simos Yannas, Mohsen Zikri, Andy Pye, David Richards, Arfon Davis, Walter Schreiber, Maria Tereza, Beatriz Elvira Fábregues, Miguel Gustavo Fábregues

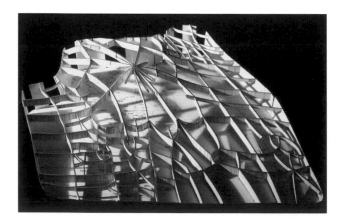

Jee Seon Lim
At the building scale, subdivision mesh algorithms are used to create a differentiated structural and panel tiling system that responds to multi-scalar topological, structural and environmental phenomena.

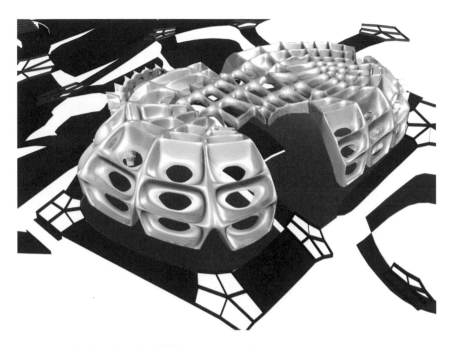

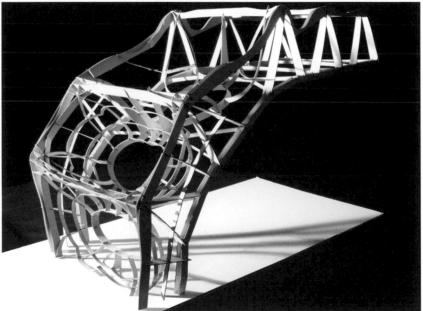

Yun Hee Choi
Above: A multi-scalar and multi-functional deployment of the devices responds to differentiating exterior solar and wind forces to create variable interior programmatic lighting effects and cooling ambiences. Below: A symbiotic environmental and structural primitive is used to promote the canalised reflection of light and wind flows to create both diffused and direct interior lighting and ventilation conditions.

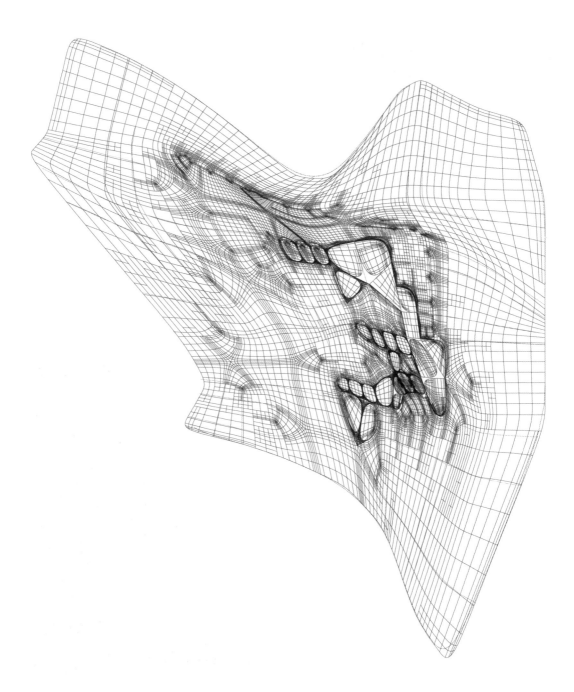

Ricky Rui Li
Above: At the macro scale, subdivision mesh algorithms are used to re-mediate eroding
canals of the site, negotiating between the competing forces of pedestrian cultural paths,
steep topography and artificial wetland network. Opposite, above: Emergent architectural
systems transfer rain into the newly formed groundwater canals and shelter a network of
cultural corridors. Opposite, below: Scooping and channelling devices create an evaporative
cooling water cascade on the facade, as well as an internal wet pipe thermal mass system.

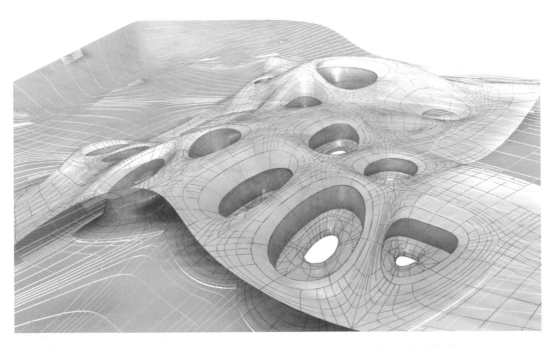

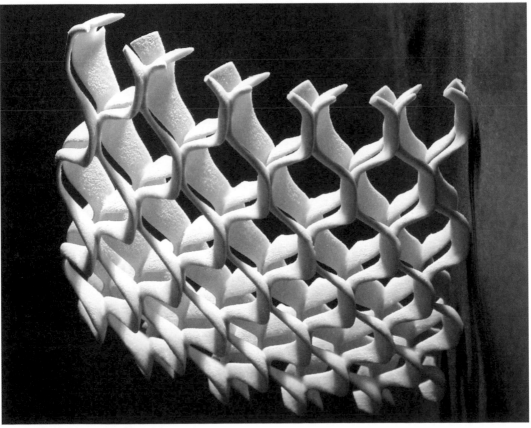

Diploma Unit 3

We took Le Corbusier's promenade on the Cote d'Azur as a time passage location, starting at the cabanon, stretching for kilometres, with Monte Carlo in the west loosely attached to Italy in the east, and overlooked by Corb's grave, high above in Cap Martin. Our purpose: to rethink and formulate new dimensions of spatiality – a roadmovie architecture. Light, Air and Duration were the building materials. Video filming and writing were the building technology.

Jean Taek Park's project detected the dynamics of water–currents and its forceful waterspray spatiality.

Diego Van Der Laat's speculation dealt with the impossibility of defining the dimensions of a line (the architect's conventional means of expression). Light is the definition tool.

Alex Chalmers' investigation circled around vertigo and the wish for extension of physical stepping out.

Unit Staff: Pascal Schöning, Rubens Azevedo, Julian Löffler

Students: Stefania Batoeva, Alex Chalmers, Timothy Dempers, Tommaso Franzolini, Noe Golomb, Emu Masuyama, Jean Taek Park, Jesse Sabatier, Nikolay Shahpazov, Diego Van Der Laat, Linjie Wang, Sophia Yetton, Nogol Zahabi

We thank Thomas Durner, Mike Weinstock, Joel Newman, Quintin Lake, Brian Hatton, William Firebrace, Ron Kenley and Jean Attali for their support.

Towards a Manifesto for Cinematic Architecture

'The very essence of cinematic architecture is nothing less than the complete transformation of solid state materialistic architecture into an energised ever changing process of illuminated and enlightening event appearances where past present and future activate a time spatiality defined by the duration perceptible through our senses and structured by our mental ability where the effect of independent movement of matter in space which is the physical kinematics is illuminated by the often contradictory revelation of filmic cinematic sequences of narrative memory procedures thus combining the otherwise impossible simultaneity of space and time.'

From *Manifesto for a Cinematic Architecture*, AA Publications, 2006

Video stills
Jaen Taek Park
Spaces of Intensities (opposite)
Diego Van Der Laat
A Speculation on the Impossibility of Defining the Dimensions of a Line (overleaf left)
Alex Chalmers
The Edge of Seduction (overleaf right)

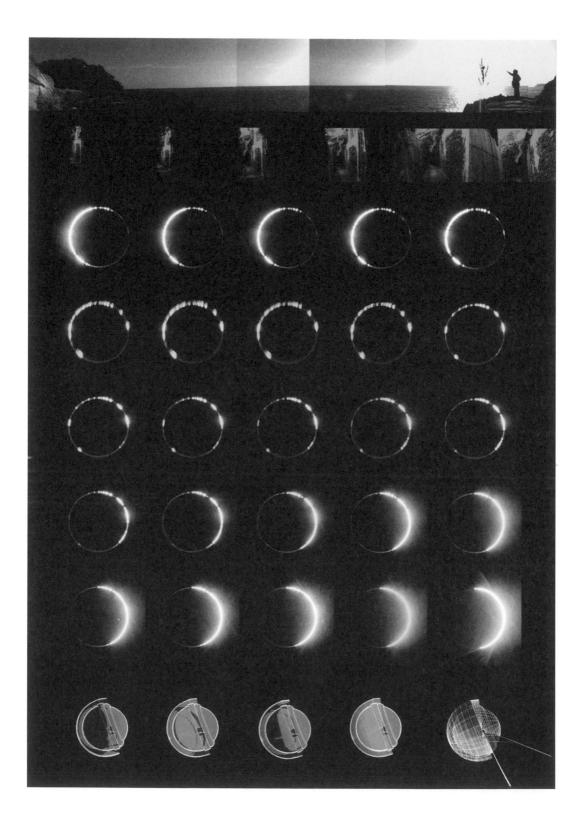

Diploma Unit 4

Morpho-Ecologies 03 —
Differentiation and Performance

Morphology is not only a study of material things and of the forms of material things, but has its dynamical aspect, under which we deal with the interpretation, in terms of force, of the operations of Energy.
D'Arcy Wentworth Thompson[1]

The cumulative effect of architecture during the last two centuries has been like that of a general lobotomy performed on society at large, obliterating vast areas of social experience. It is employed more and more as a preventive measure; an agency ... which by its very nature limits the horizon of experience.
Robin Evans[2]

This year Dip 4 completed the third year of its Morpho-Ecological research programme, which investigates the dynamic relation between morphologies, morphogenesis and ecologies. More specifically, Morpho-Ecology describes spatial strategies, material systems, environmental modulation and the opportunities for inhabitation of the built environment that arise from this dynamic relation. The book *Morpho-Ecologies: Towards an Inclusive Discourse on Heterogeneous Space in Architecture* (AA Publications, London, 2006) elaborates the research. See also differentiatedstructures.net (to be launched this summer).

[1] *On Growth and Form: A New Edition*; Cambridge University Press, 1942
[2] 'Figures, Doors and Passages'; in *Translations from Drawing to Building and Other Essays*, AA Publications, 1997

Unit Staff: Michael Hensel, Achim Menges

Students: Louis Gadd, Caroline Grübel, Omid Kamvari, Asif Amir Khan, Julia King, Dae Song Lee, Mustasha Musa, Gabriel Sanchiz Garin, Pavlos Sideris, Defne Sunguroglu, Gen Takahashi

Dip 4 would like to thank
Phil Ayres, Simon Beames, Mark Burry, Daniel Coll I Capdevila, Ludo Grooteman, Martin Hemberg, Christopher Hight, Aleksandra Jäschke, Prof George Jeronimidis, Sean Lally, Theo Lorenz, Frei Otto, Eva Scheffler, Pascal Schöning, Patrik Schumacher, Bob Sheil, Brett Steele, Juan Subercaseaux, Peter Trummer, Jeffrey Turko, Prof Julian Vincent, Michael Weinstock, Simos Yannas

At AHO IFID: Steinar Killi, Birger Sevaldson

At HfG Offenbach: Peter Eckart, Peter Esselbrügge, Wolfgang Heide
At Buro Happold: Mike Cook, Jalal El-Ali, Lawrence Friesen, Nikolaos Stathopoulos, Wolf Mangelsdorf

At Bentley Systems and the Smart Geometry Group: Robert Aish, Francis Aish, Kaustuv DeBiswas, Lars Hasselgren, Roly Hudson, Axel Kilian, Hugh Whitehead, Chris Williams, Rob Woodbury

At the Federal University of Pernambuco: Jose Zeca Brandao

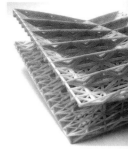

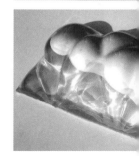

Left: Morphologies – various rapid prototype and cast models that investigate different aspects of the material systems in development, including geometry, porosity, modulation of the luminous environment and elastic limit.

Below: Performance – fluid dynamics analysis on a region of a material system to examine the airflow modulation relative to differentiated porosity of the system.

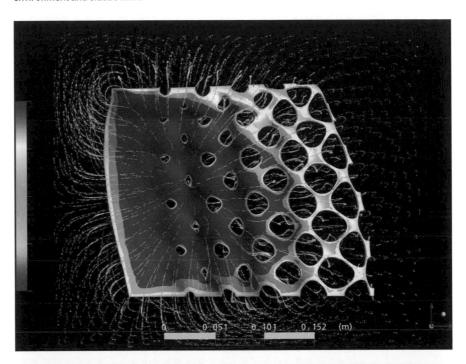

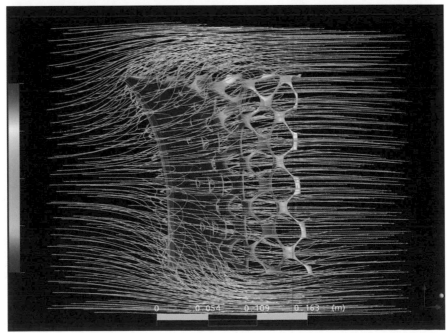

Left: Environment – combinatory map configured in an associative modelling environment and linked to an Excel spreadsheet. Numerical changes in the spreadsheet automatically update the map, which shows airflow conditions, illuminance and temperature measurements across 20,000 measure points distributed over a site in Bairro de Recife.

This page: Various full-scale prototypes that examine spatial arrangement and environmental modulation capacities of the developed material systems.

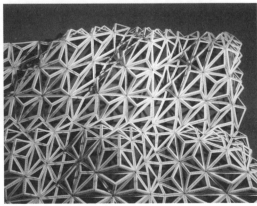

Diploma Unit 6

At the heart of Dip 6's investigation is the rethinking of the affect of types beyond their immediate singular and architectural scale, where types are understood as a collective urban entity that holds the potential to seed, differentiate, regulate and administer the urban plan.

Our questioning of the addictive reliance on the staging and proliferation of landmarks necessitates a rethinking of new urban developments that goes beyond the iconic and the potentials that dominant types exert on an urban plan.

We realised that to begin to rethink and thus re-envision a dominant type in an urban plan inevitably raises questions of control, flexibility, difference and participation – and most acutely the need to address the issue of programmatic afterlives, the capacity for self-renewal or reconfiguration in order to elude eventual expiry and maintain sustainability. This subsequently posed the fundamental question of where architecture stops and urbanism begins. Does relinquishing total control over an urban plan mean abdicating responsibility for urbanity? And if so, what tools are available to sustain typological control and freedom?

Amongst the possibilities we discovered this year were typological structures with an elastic nature that allows for typological transitions, renewal and reconfiguration within and across themselves. At the opposite end of the scale, we explored the potential of the structured ground to create a differentiated and robust typological fabric. To enable and choreograph these findings we devised what we contingently term a 'typological guideline' (as opposed to an 'urban design guideline') as a tool of representation and projection across scales and ambitions.

Unit Staff: Chris Lee, Sam Jacoby

Seminars and Workshops:
Lawrence Barth, Hanif Kara & AKT, Kelvin Chu, Homin Kim

Students: Elfreda Chan, Shin Hyung Cho, Catharina Frankander, Sheau-Fei Hoe, Minseok Kim, Keong Wee Lim, Yi Cheng Pan, Rachael Scarr-Hall, Valeria Segovia Trigueros, Erez Shani, Max von Werz

Jurors: Leyre Asensio, Rubens Azevedo, Katharina Borsi, Carlos Villanueva Brandt, Alan Dempsey, Markus Dietling, Shin Egashira, Ridzwa Fathan, Stephen Hardy, Michael Hensel, Hugo Hinsley, Francesca Hughes, Christian Hutter, Michael Kirchmann, David Mah, Yusuke Obuchi, Stephen Rowe, Irénée Scalbert, Brett Steele, Charles Tashima, Tom Verebes, Ellis Woodman

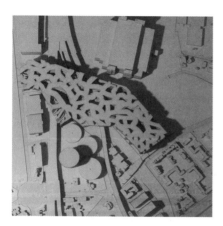

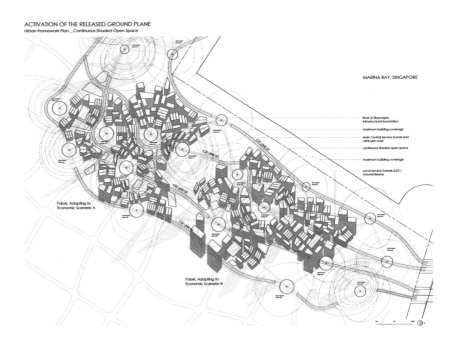

ACTIVATION OF THE RELEASED GROUND PLANE
Urban Framework Plan _ Continuous Shaded Open Space

MARINA BAY, SINGAPORE

Yi Cheng Pan
Resisting the Genetic Empire, Manila Bay, Singapore
The proliferation of the homogeneous skyscraper is counteracted by a strategy of intensifying
control of the type.

Left: Valeria Segovia Trigueros
Interiorised Urbanism, Battersea Power Station, London
The project studies two ways of compressing programme within a collective type: the Megatype.

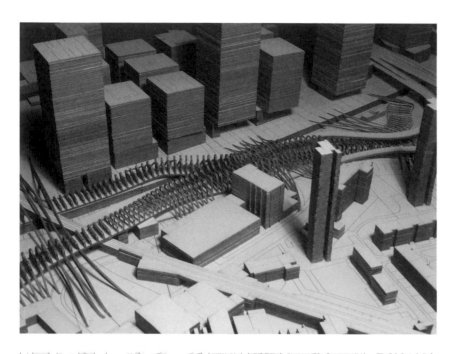

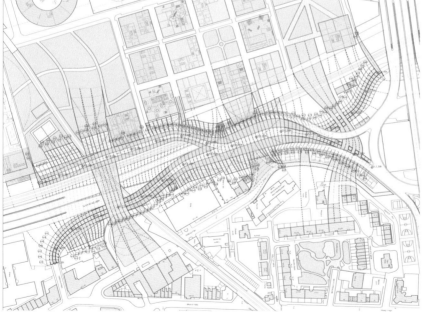

Max von Werz
Projective Arcade, White City, London
A series of highly localised and inclusive arcades are deployed along
the periphery of OMA's White City masterplan in order to consolidate
conflicting edge conditions and reclaim desolate strips of redundant
spaces left over by large-scale transportation infrastructure.

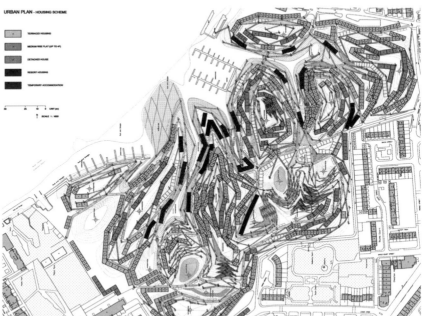

Minseok Kim
Multiple Public Ground, Thames Gateway, Deptford
Over the next 30 years it is anticipated that global warming will cause
water levels to rise, erasing large areas of existing public land. This
suggests the need for new planning strategies that integrate water
management and accommodate the emergence of new building types.

Diploma Unit 8

Diploma Unit 8 sets a research agenda into the nature of our experience of architecture. We take the weather as a starting point, asking not what causes it, how to simulate it or what impact it has on buildings, but what it is like to be immersed in the weather and how those sensations might be reoriginated in built material. Taking the hypothesis that affect resides in material, how can the goal of achieving a particular affect dictate new ways of organising material, and how can new ways of using material generate new affects?

In fog there is no geography, no point of reference. In a blizzard we occupy an intimate space that extends infinitely.... The research of the unit develops techniques to actualise these and other affects materially. An instrumental use of material allows precise control and tuning of affects. In parallel to this stream of investigation, related systematic research explored the potential of virtual sets of relations derived from meteorological models to choreograph affects – 'abstract machines' – which allow complex virtual relations to emerge. A series of feedback loops established within the process assessed design strategies against research agendas continuously.

A unit trip to Hong Kong exposed us to the very local intensities of the contemporary global city. On returning to London we developed notation techniques to capture and gauge these evanescent qualities, using these notations to recompose the moods of the city and as inputs to our abstract machines. Finally, these recomposed effects are actualised on site using our material systems to create new moods, new atmospheres and new affects in the city.

Unit Staff: Chiafang Wu, Stephen Roe

Workshops: Nikolaos Stathopoulos, Andrew Stiff at D-Fuse

Students: Mei Chan, Billy Choi, Minaki Goto, Francois Guyot, Antonis Karides, Emmanouela Koutentaki, Henry Leung, Edwin Tam, Alicia Tan

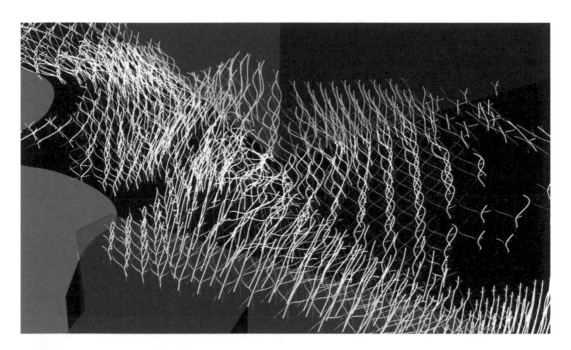

Billy Choi
Kowloon Blizzard
The sensation of being in a blizzard is characterised by drastically reduced yet ever–changing visibility conditions, and the intimacy of being surrounded by an infinite field of blowing snow. This project recreates the blizzard experience by means of an extensive material field, manipulating vision and creating detours and discoveries in an otherwise undifferentiated public space.

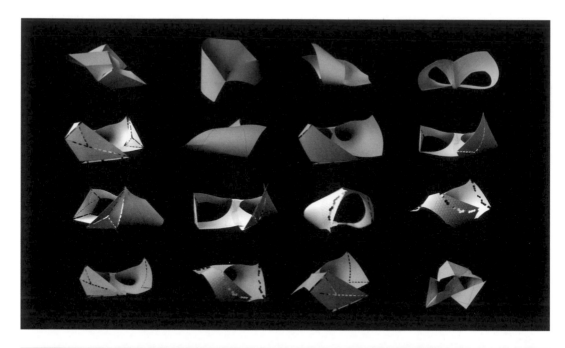

Top: Francois Guyot
Tiled Confusion
Development of a Moebius-strip tile to be proliferated 3-dimensionally

Bottom: Henry Leung
Aggregation of Light
Creating new moods and atmospheres in the alleyways of Hong Kong

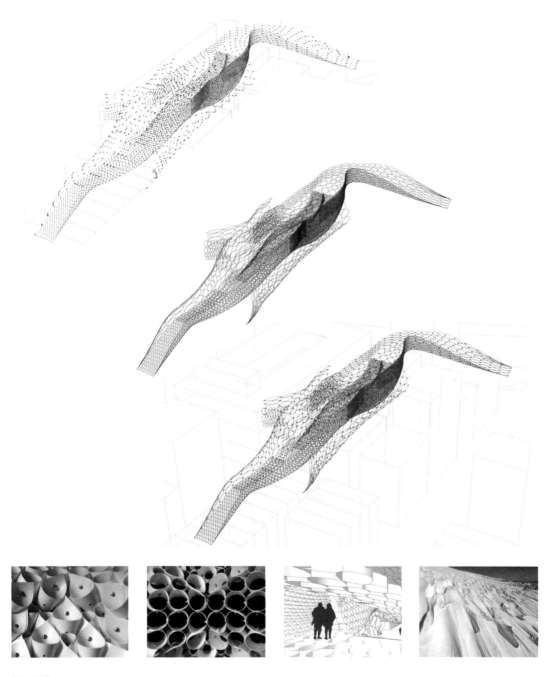

Minaki Goto
Snow Particle Landscape
Starting with multiple scales – from snowflake to snowscape –
the project re-originates these effects within one material system.
Fields of particle-like connectors control the arraying of a variable
modular system in space, accumulating into new landscapes in the city.
These new landscapes provide new connections while their fluctuating
visual quality maintains privacy or encourages openness.

Diploma Unit 9

This year the unit conducted research into thresholds between architecture, media arts and urban design. Given that architecture articulates its practices through meta-programmes, each enacted through codified systems of representation, cultural and techno-logical imperatives demand continual re-evaluation of these systems, both as didactic and illustrative instruments. The defining quality of the unit's research is therefore embodied in its methodology, where critical engage-ment with the tools of data-gathering and design development act recursively. Working between hardware and soft-ware components, it has been the task of the unit to explore the potentials for architecture which contemporary physical/electronic hybrid systems appear to promise.

One Fourth Year and one Fifth Year project have been chosen to illustrate the scope of the unit's work; each is introduced here by their authors.

Unit Staff: John Bell, Adam Covell

Students: Kin Man Kevin Ling, Hlanganiso Killion Mokwete, Rajat Sodhi, Ekapob Suksudpaisarn, Mohammad Iskand Abdul Razak, Yumeng Chan, Toby Maloy, Pavandeep Singh Panesar, Chris Wong

Critics, Collaborators and Consultants: Betaminds, Nic Clear, Alistair Gill, Pete Gomes, Usman Haque, Jennifer Harvey, Alex Haw, Lorens Holm, Holger Kehne, Theo Lorenz, Volker Morawe, Sean Pickersgill, Charles Tashima, Mark Tynan, John Wynne, Michel'Angelo Ziccarelli

The unit would like to thank Colm Lally and Chloe Viatsou from E:vent for their generous help and support.

Ekapob Suksudpaisarn, Fourth Year
An attempt to create an autonomous representation of building that is for and of itself and free from any narrative context. The programme provides a temporary space for private event and public space to initiate wider engagement with the diversity of London fashion and design culture. The approach is to generate the proposal through negotiation between specific viewpoints, environments and discourses.

Right: Camera paths' focal lengths and view angles developed through programmatic analysis of the event act as spatial precursors for envelope generation. Below: Dynamic mapping of camera match-moving.

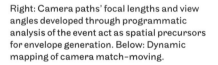

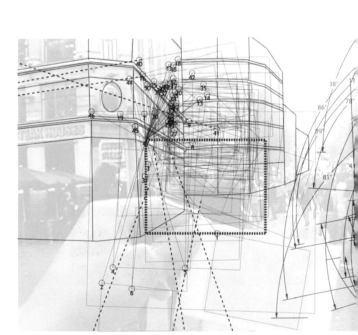

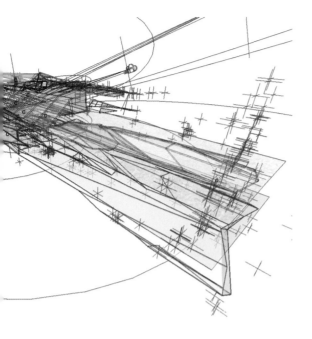

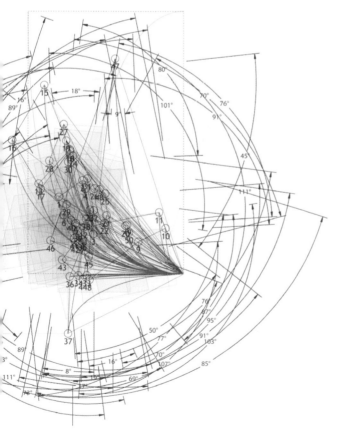

Below, top: *What is Home?*
E:vent 12.05: Toby Maloy, Chris Wong,
Hlanganiso Mokwete
Time-delay still from the presentation of
work resulting from a three-week residency
at the E:vent Gallery in December 2005.
Proximity sensors trigger spatialised sound
taken from interviews answering the question
'what is home?' The dwell times of visitors in
the space are recorded to a database for later
evaluation.

Bottom two images: *Threshold*, a group show
at E:vent gallery in April 2006 where the unit
collaborated with invited media artists Volker
Morawe and John Wynne.

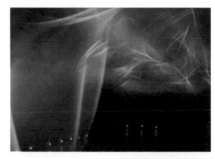

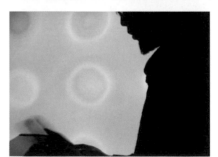

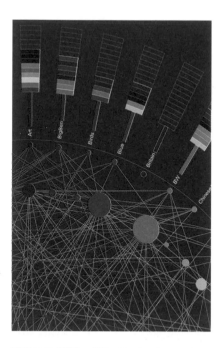

Toby Maloy, Fifth Year
Transient perspectile moments address
the role of the public within public spaces,
critically analysing the consumption of
monuments through photographic
media. This proposal for a new square,
where public programmes can exist
without the dominance of the photographic gaze, would allow new relationships to form. The space rewards the
users involved in collective engagement
by establishing dynamic anamorphic
views of the original monuments of
Trafalgar Square, providing a highly
specific dynamic viewpoint.

This page: Mapping of Flickr-tagged photographs within Trafalgar Square. Dominant
views and shot positions are overlaid.
Opposite page: Anamorphic devices replace
Nelson's Column and fountains, with
previsualisation of elements (above) and final
scheme below.

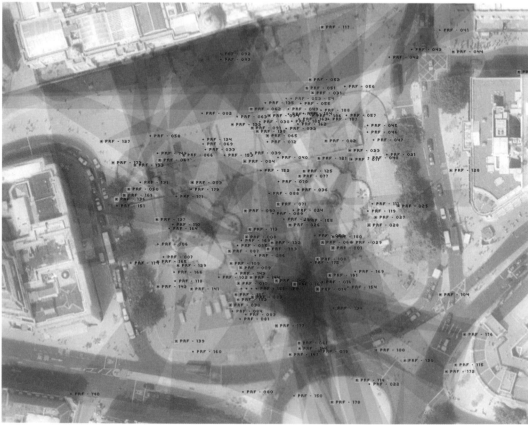

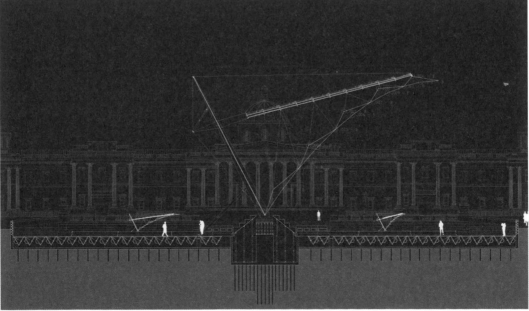

Diploma Unit 10

Direct Urbanism

Diploma 10 has developed 10 individual concepts for direct urbanism. It compared two working London sites in order to isolate, unravel and define the principles that make up the live realm of the city. The first site, Nine Elms, was interpreted as 'operative' and the second, which was individually chosen, was interpreted as 'active'. It worked from a process of immersion to a process of insertion. In immersion, it inhabited and participated in the active and operative sites, modelled and compared the two sites and chose, defined and constructed a territory of action. In insertion, it interacted with the territory of action, designed an architectural application (urban architecture), designed an urban application (architectural urbanism) and proposed a composite, active and operative urban strategy that generated the 10 individual interpretations of direct urbanism.

Other Direct Urbanisms

01 – The Cross River Tram: Activating an infrastructural line, Alinda Barua; 02 – Save Energy?, Tim Owen den Dekker; 03 – Developing Six Initiatives to Activate an Operative Site, Carl Fraser; 05 – The Distracted City, Magnea Gudmundsdottir; 06 – Urban Appropriation, Lewis Kinneir; 07 – Urban Behavioural Modification: Operative responses to active situations, Anna Mansfield; 09 – Urban Decanting, Chris Thorn

Unit Master: Carlos Villanueva Brandt

Students: Alinda Barua, Tim Owen den Dekker, Carl Fraser, Christina Godiksen, Magnea Gudmundsdottir, Lewis Kinneir, Anna Mansfield, Chris Smith, Chris Thorn, Alex Warnock–Smith

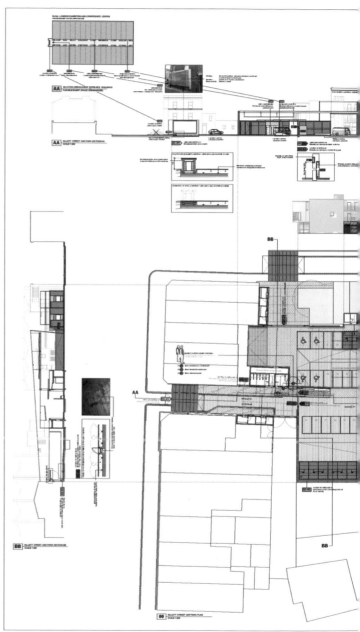

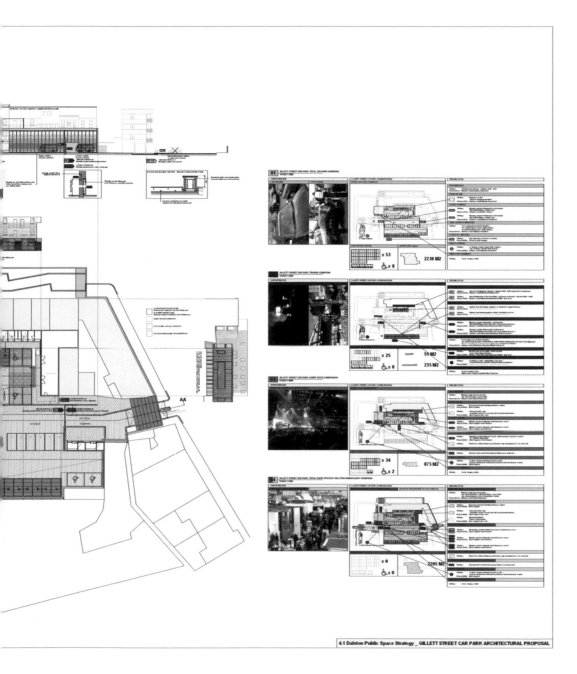

4.1 Dalston Public Space Strategy _ GILLETT STREET CAR PARK ARCHITECTURAL PROPOSAL

08 Chris Smith
Direct Urbanism = Temporary Public Space
The project questions the current approach to public space development within the Mayor's 'Making Space for Londoners' programme. Proposals are developed that can support a timetabled social reuse to create an alternative temporary public realm. Three key spaces, linked by Kingsland High Street, are identified as sites for intervention: Ridley Road Street Market, Gillett Street Car Park and Bentley Street Car Park. Infrastructural elements, additional services and access control activate the two car parks while retaining their original function. At the urban scale, the three individual sites can be linked territorially and socially by means of a Dalston-wide event.

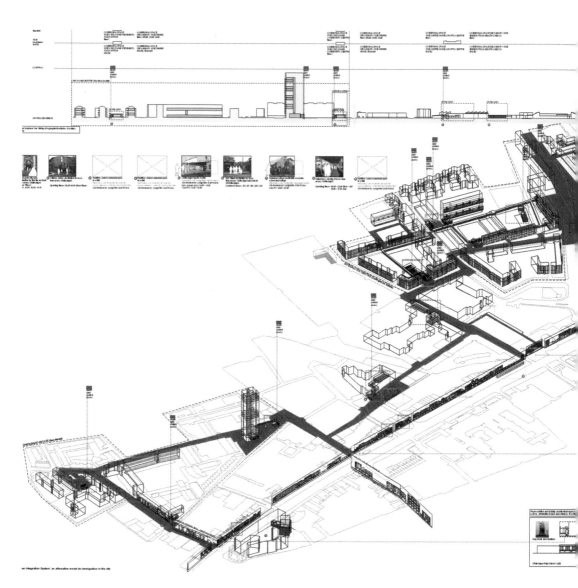

10 Alex Warnock-Smith (above)
Direct Urbanism = Urban Integration System
Examining the experience of the immigration system for arriving
asylum seekers, and the social, cultural and spatial conditions of
developing immigrant communities in Whitechapel, the project
overlays the immigration system on the city and uses it as a mechanism
for urban change. An urban integration system is proposed to link
segregated communities and territories, and to distribute services for
arriving asylum seekers. In line with the transfer of Tower Hamlets
Council Housing to Specialist Housing Associations, Collingwood
Estate is redesigned as an alternative architectural typology, the
Integration Centre that provides a dispersed and integrated alternative
to the Detention Centre.

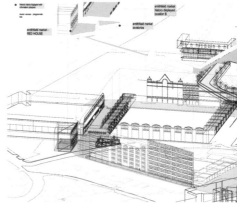

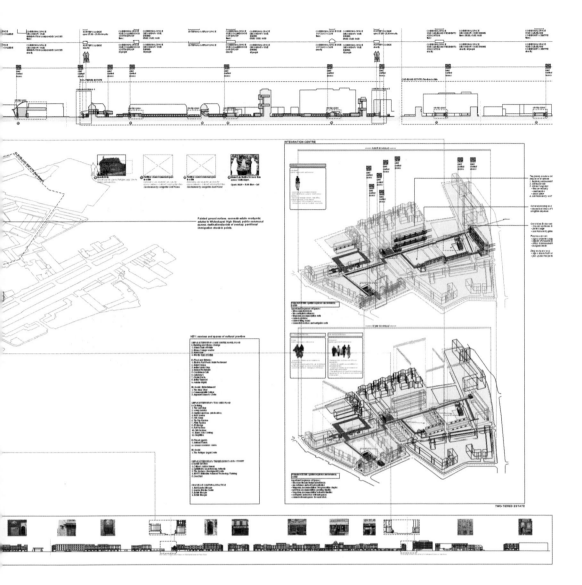

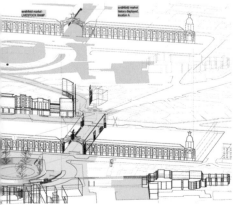

04 Christina Godiksen (left)

Direct Urbanism = Facilitating Self-Organised Urbanism

The site is the Smithfield area of the City of London. Through investigations, examples and a series of proposals, the project identifies the value of facilitating self-organised urbanism as an active mechanism that extends the perception of public space. Self-organised urbanism encourages a positive use of the city by providing self-organised public services, extending access to public space and reclaiming abandoned structures. The hypothesis is that self-organised urbanism can work in conjunction with existing urban forces to reduce obsolescence in the city fabric and moderate the economic and operational pressures on the public realm by distributing responsibility and control.

Diploma Unit 11

Three stages of experiments this year began with direct sampling of urban residues in the area surrounding Battersea Power Station. We produced a guidebook, 'Made in Battersea', which contains a collection of urban resources. The chosen sampling zone includes New Covent Garden Market, a concrete and gravel yard, a waste transfer station, Battersea Dogs Home and 112 spin-off sites from intersections of viaducts and 80 light industries. The guidebook indicates their location and quantitative data, and also illustrates methods of re-utilising these potential urban resources through the technique of collage and bricolage. At Hooke Park each student constructed models of Urban Vehicles at a scale between that of toys and street furniture. The vehicles were further developed as a means of cross-utilisation between excess materials and gaps between systems, inhabiting the notional fields that have been contextualised through 'Made in Battersea'. Our final proposals explored further applications of our vehicles as urban facilities that demarcate informal territories; it is this form of interference and play that we would like our vehicles to coordinate: bodies of architecture without space, bodily infrastructure of the city in a constant state of flux.

Unit Master: Shin Egashira

Students: Mario Gottfried, Kazunobu Hayasaki, Robert Luck, Orlando Oliver, III-Sam Park, Krishan Pattni, Ivana Sehik, Robin Sjöholm, Alex Tsangarides, Iris Wong, Mo Wong

Thanks to: Theo Jansen, Panamarenko, Nicholas Boyarsky, Raoul Bunschoten, Peter Carl, Charles Corry Wright, David Greene, Francesca Hughes, Andreas Lang, Chris Lee, Kuwan Guan Lee, George L Legendre, Theo Lorenz, Matthew Murphy, Yusuke Obuchi, Fred Scott, Martina Schäfer, Pete Silver, Theo Spyropoulos, Carlos Villanueva Brandt, AA Workshop, Brett Steele

1

2

3

4

5

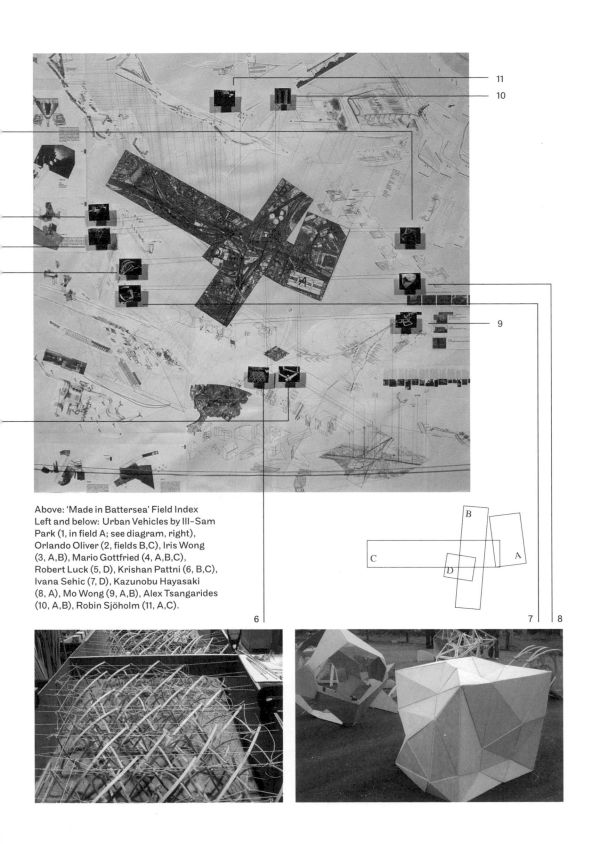

Above: 'Made in Battersea' Field Index
Left and below: Urban Vehicles by Ill–Sam
Park (1, in field A; see diagram, right),
Orlando Oliver (2, fields B,C), Iris Wong
(3, A,B), Mario Gottfried (4, A,B,C),
Robert Luck (5, D), Krishan Pattni (6, B,C),
Ivana Sehic (7, D), Kazunobu Hayasaki
(8, A), Mo Wong (9, A,B), Alex Tsangarides
(10, A,B), Robin Sjöholm (11, A,C).

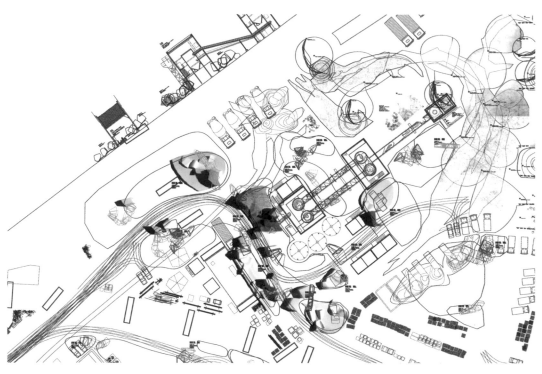

Ivana Sehic
Dynamic Architecture in a Stable Frame
The project is used to animate and choreograph dead spaces. It is tested in Battersea, where the speed of growth and lack of planning produced a chaotic place of strange adjacencies. The area that gives timetable and space to this architecture is a former locomotive repair workshop. With placement of new objects, the site becomes at places faster, at times slower, sometimes difficult, sometimes smooth. New architecture exists between found spaces.

III-Sam Park, *Interactive Waterscape*
The project explores artificial landscape
which coordinates and negotiates
dynamic operational flux and events in
water-dependent industries in Nine Elms,
Battersea, through various water spaces
controlled by interactive water beds.
It attempts to open up the non-public
industrial realm to the public by
examining water treatment as a new type
of inhabitable organisational structure
which introduces a new notion of time by
slow water purification, manifested
through a series of spatial conditions.

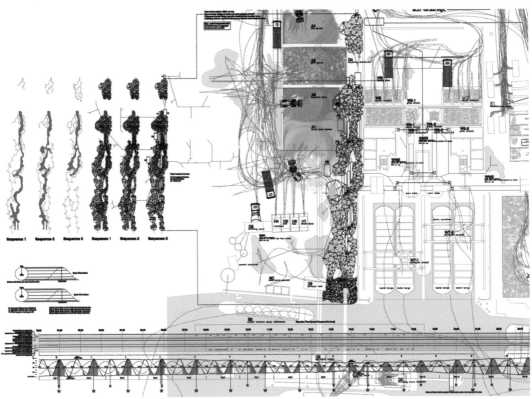

Diploma Unit 12

Diploma Unit 12 is concerned with the development of new modes of practice that engage the strategic social, political and structural parameters which continuously reconfigure the city. We favour neither form nor programme but focus on the reciprocities and interrelationships between the two, expressed at every environmental scale, from the global, via the regional, to the scale of individual experience. One such example for this practice is Nikolaus Wabnitz's Parametric Lichen. Birmingham's Gravelly Hill Interchange (Spaghetti Junction) sits above the city with the problem of traffic flow its sole programmatic concern. This 1960s motorway interchange is a product of the modernist urban paradigm that fragments the city's flows — transport, leisure, work, communication — so that each is forced to take place in a mono-functional vacuum. In this abstracted dimension, space is made quantitatively productive but qualitatively impoverished, and as much as the junction solves one problem it creates another in the barren non-spaces that lurk beneath it.

The project proposes a connective strategy to address this disjunctive condition. Interwoven between the existing structure and the urban fabric, a new system will establish a series of nodal intensities through which the city's various flows can connect and new conditions emerge. The relations between large-scale infrastructure, local inhabitation and landscape are parametrically reconfigured to perform as a non-hierarchical, tissue-like formation. Within this strategy conditions such as the noise and light emitted by traffic are not treated as problems to be negated, but as factors which can be adapted to create spaces with differing environmental qualities. These spaces then operate as attractors, forming pockets of intensity within the tissue from which a network of public activity might flow.

Unit Staff: Eva Castro, Holger Kehne

Technical Tutor: Raymond Lau

Students: Francesco Brenta, Yonosuke Fukuda, Federico Rossi, Nikolaus Wabnitz, Jan Wisniowski

Consultants: Benedikt Schleicher – Arup, Douglas Spencer, Rebecca Haines – Gadd, Eduardo Luzzatto – Giuliani_Gehry Tech, Marco Poletto – EcoLogic studio, Gabriel Duarte

With thanks to: John Bell, Rita Lambert, Francesca Hughes, Yusuke Obuchi, Antonia Loyd, Belinda Flaherty, Marilyn Dyer, Brett Steele, Jeff Turko, Robert Thum, Claudia Pasquero, Karola Dierichs

Above: Iterative simulation of accumulative distortions along splines.

Right: Birmingham's Gravelly Hill Interchange (Spaghetti Junction).

Top: Parametric catalogue of varied configurations using angle, depth and density as variables to control spatial porosity

Bottom: Catia testing_variation of parameters.

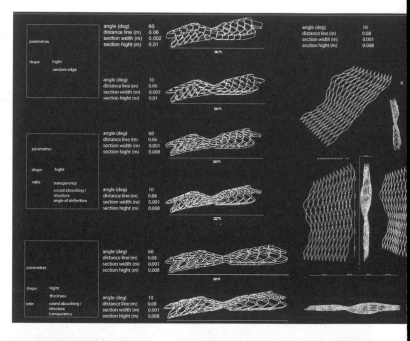

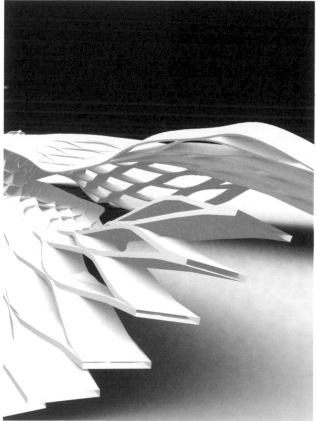

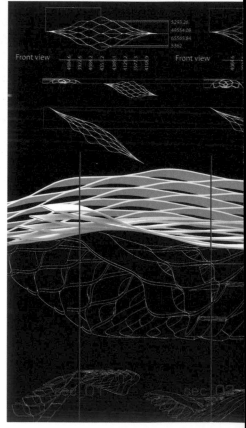

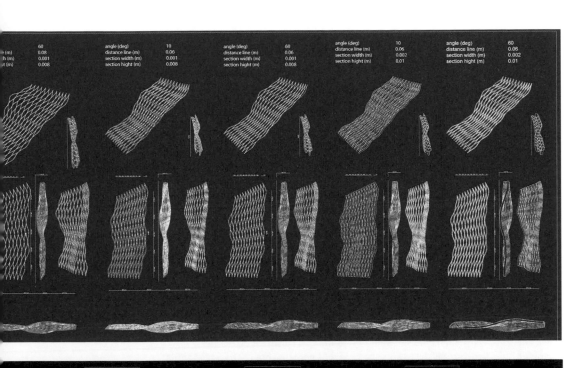

		angle (deg)	10	angle (deg)	60	angle (deg)	10	angle (deg)	60
	60	distance line (m)	0.06	distance line (m)	0.06	distance line (m)	0.06	distance line (m)	0.06
	0.08	section width (m)	0.001	section width (m)	0.001	section width (m)	0.002	section width (m)	0.002
	0.001	section hight (m)	0.008	section hight (m)	0.008	section hight (m)	0.01	section hight (m)	0.01
	0.008								

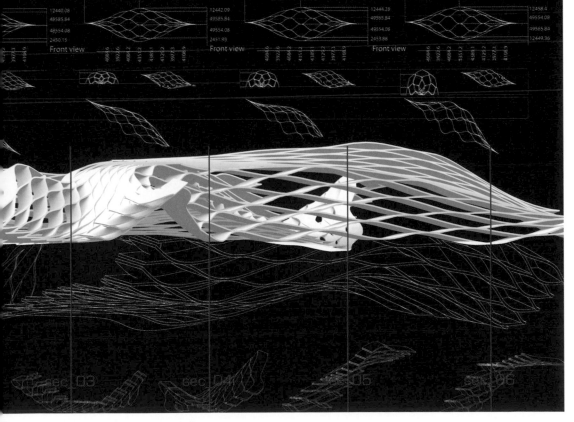

Diploma Unit 13

Architecture as time and space shift

Today, globalisation and climatic disturbance – two of the most important mutations of the beginning of the twenty-first century – have engendered a deep transformation of the notions of space and time. Architecture deploys itself in a henceforth universal space, projecting without discontinuity an eternal continuous present that is invariable, everywhere the same, always there. The continuum creates spatiality and temporality extending beyond biological cycles, without sleep or season, outside of astronomical and climatic rhythms, without night or winter, without rain or chill. Information is instantaneous, connections simultaneous, and the communications network is global, without interruption. Here and now, but also over there and tomorrow, all meteorological variables have been stabilised to an average of shared comfort: somewhere around 21°C, relative humidity at 50%, light intensity at 1000 lux, like a beautiful spring day in London that we have decided to repeat infinitely, all over the world.

Our unit brings a critical agenda to this existing situation. In this eternal climatic homogeneity, we are looking for an architecture that would enable us to articulate this continuum, an instrument to create fault-lines, ruptures and fog, making certain climates swell punctually or momentarily, naturalising a context or on the contrary distancing it even more, creating moments, generating meteorologies, projecting seasons and times, spatialising functions, shortening or amplifying distances, diminishing the length of the day or creating an endless night, here and there, out of time and space. The journey is instantaneous, from one climate to another, from one geographical location to another.

Our unit seeks an architecture which proceeds by way of space-time distortions, working on the very matter of space and time, using slips, shifts, accelerations and contractions. By going beyond the traditional metric and volumetric frame, our unit wishes to extend the field of architecture to new dimensions, working in the spectrum of the void and the density of the body, in the folds of time, the warping of distances and climates. Architecture proceeds by way of climatic and temporal modification. It generates a whole host of temporary local breaks, geographical breaches, astronomical shifts, and temporal contractions.

Within this context, we have attempted to redesign London's proposed artificial beach on the South Bank this summer, pursuing architectures that eschew traditional entertainments for deeper distortions.

Unit Staff: Philippe Rahm, Alex Haw

Students: Maximilian Beckenbauer, Antonios Daikos, Eli Hatleskog, Daniel Koo, Yuki Namba, Fred Pittman, Takao Shimizu

Workshops: Monia De Marchi, Eugene Han, Simos Yannas

Jurors: Denis Balent, Shumon Basar, John Bell, Josh Bolchover, Peter Carl, Francesca Hughes, Sam Jacob, Sam Jacoby, Holger Kehne, Nate Kolbe, Dominik Kremerskothen, Chris Lee, Franklin Lee, Jonas Lundberg, Yusuke Obuchi, Martina Schäfer, Pascal Schöning, Brett Steele, Tom Verebes, Carlos Villanueva Brandt, Tom Weaver

Opposite: Eli Hatleskog
Large visitor numbers are a feature of the South Bank and these bodies are powered by food. People require power to fuel movement and this is supplied, on site, by numerous hotdog and burger vendors. But what does one burger fuel exactly? An hour of jogging or three of sleeping? The human body is constantly losing energy, when muscles move, to its surroundings, in the form of heat.

Energy leaves a person in accordance with temperature differential, surface area and activity levels. So the aim of this project is to create an environment in which the energy levels are tampered with, so one may consume energy, say in the form of a burger, and it then affects one's appreciation of a given space.

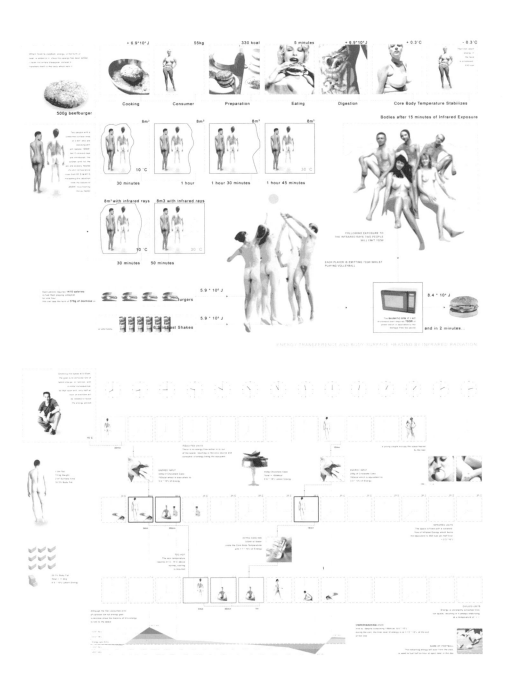

Put simply, if I eat too much, I sweat and, in turn, that heats the area in which I stand. So, how far can I run with this energy before it is given to the air? And, is it possible to eat a kilogram of chocolate at 2pm yet leave the beach at 4pm without a trace of the calories consumed? In effect, a place is created which steals and preserves heat, or energy in transit, so that one may consume without consequence.

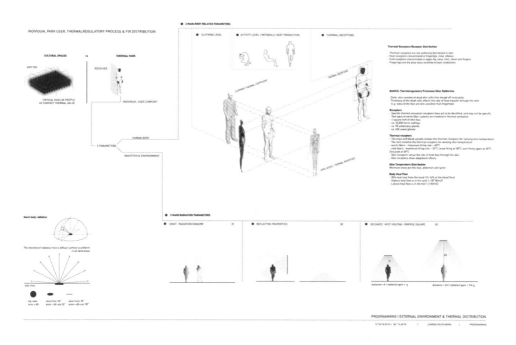

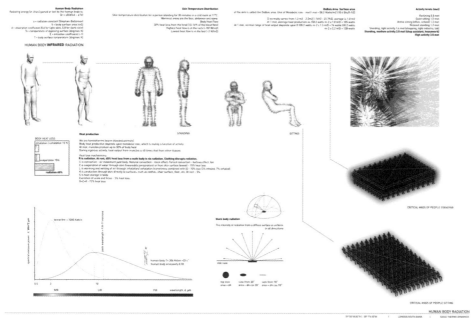

Maximilian Beckenbauer

'Open South Bank' is a direct response to two current developments of the unit's chosen site: Hungerford car park, located between the Royal Festival Hall and Jubilee Gardens, South Bank. The proposal for the temporary London Beach is considered in the context of the long-running planning dispute over the permanent development plans for this 'key' site: Cultural Complex vs. Park.

By superimposing the two opposed, unimaginative positions, and changing their rigid parameters, the project aims to mediate between the environments climatically. It invents an architectural material system that manages to negotiate the radiant transfer of metabolic heat produced by human bodies between two distinct places. This creates enclosed cultural

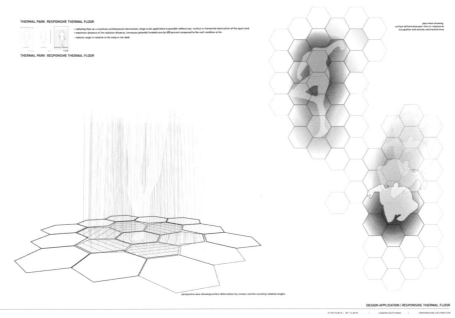

spaces which give off the thermal energy created by one set of users (those in favour of extending the cultural complex) to feed a thermal park and with it the other set of (pro open space) users around the cultural enclosures. By making considered compromises on both positions and linking them with each other, a new typology of architecture is created that leads to new programming possibilities. The changing external conditions forge a seasonal programming of cultural events which respond to London's changing climatic conditions, and relate body masses to cultural programme.

Diploma Unit 14

Diploma Unit 14 explored and revealed dynamic networks of the London Thames Gateway, the biggest urban development in Europe. Maintaining a collaborative link to political bodies (GLA), local communities and experts (Buro Happold), the students developed applied projects related to sociopolitical, infrastructural and environmental issues. During various workshops, public fora and exhibitions in London and abroad, the projects were tested and represented to enable informed feedback. Through interactive prototypes and events, the unit simultaneously instrumentalised and politicised consultation, communication and design strategies for developments in the Thames Gateway. This new typology of architectural representation led to proposals within the network which are considered as evolving formations rather than mere form.

Unit Staff: Theo Lorenz, Peter Staub, Neil Davidson

Students: Max Babbé, Esi Carboo, Alex Catterall, Nausica Gabrielides, Ioanna Ioannidis, Levent Kerimol, Celina Martinez–Canavate, Richa Mukhia, Paula Nascimento, Alex Thomas, Abigail Tuttle

Special thanks to Irene Gallou, Joel Newman, Mike Weinstock, Sue Barr, Valerie Bennett, Vanessa Norwood, Simone Sagi, Lee Regan, Mark Tynan, Antonia Loyd, Belinda Flaherty, Marilyn Dyer

Diploma Unit 14 in association with Buro Happold
Specialists: Solveig Sellers, Kien Hoang, Dina Koutsikouri, Rachna Gupta, Alasdair Young, Pablo Izquirdo, Andrew Cripps, Salmaan Craig, Elmar Hess, Chris Woodfield, Athena Papadopoulou

Supported by Brompton Bicycles Ltd, BuckleyGrayYeoman, Dar Al Handasah UK, MOOARC, Sonangol

In partnership with GLA Architecture + Urbanism Unit: Tobias Goevert & Jamie Dean ETH Zurich MAS: Prof Marc Angélil & Andrew Whiteside

Jurors: Lawrence Barth, John Bell, Katharina Borsi, Beth Bourrelly, Paulo Cossu, Monia De Marchi, Shin Egashira, Steve Hardy, Michael Hensel, Teresa Hoskyns, Richard Howarth, Andreas Lang, Franklin Lee, Jonas Lundberg, Achim Menges, Sandra Morris, Ifeanyi Oganwu, Emerson Roberts, Anne Save de Beaurecueil, Neven Sidor, Charles Tashima, Adam Tarr, Brett Steele, Carlos Villanueva Brandt, Patrick Walls, Simos Yannas, Matt Yeoman

Max Babbé
The project reassemblesinformation infrastructure technologies to create active political space for the proposed Thames Gateway Bridge. With an interest in the ongoing public consultation process and the increasing presence of interactive technologies in our culture, it attempts to make visible the space created by measuring and viewing technologies.
Opposite page, top: Views of 'Forum 1: Architects in Residence' installation at AA in November.
Opposite page, bottom: Mediation of threshold between the bridge and its surroundings.

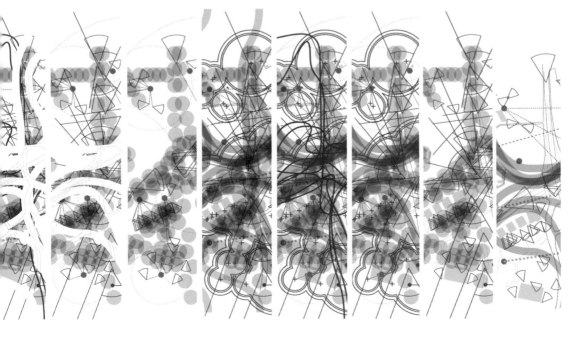

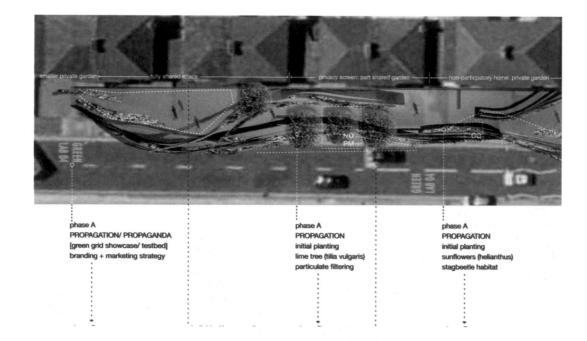

phase A
PROPAGATION/ PROPAGANDA
[green grid showcase/ testbed]
branding + marketing strategy

phase A
PROPAGATION
initial planting
lime tree (tilia vulgaris)
particulate filtering

phase A
PROPAGATION
initial planting
sunflowers (helianthus)
stagbeetle habitat

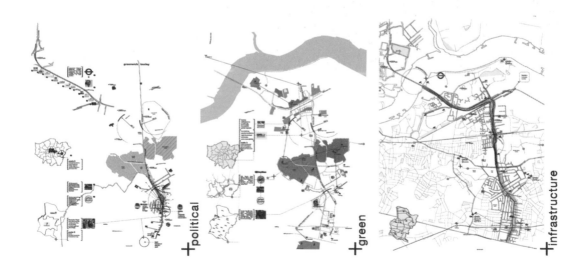

+political

+green

+infrastructure

Richa Mukhia
A strategy for the extension of the Green Grid in East London, which uses the proposed Thames
Gateway Bridge and Brompton Road (headquarters for the community protest against the
bridge) as the catalyst for the investigations, in the process creating a multi-layered habitat
of green solutions to various political and physical problems. The proposed green corridor
negotiates between the different agents and concerns involved: from the local communities
and traffic to the requirements of hibernating bats. The project aims to make the design of the
Green Grid – and its potential – public from the outset, enabling participation in its extension.

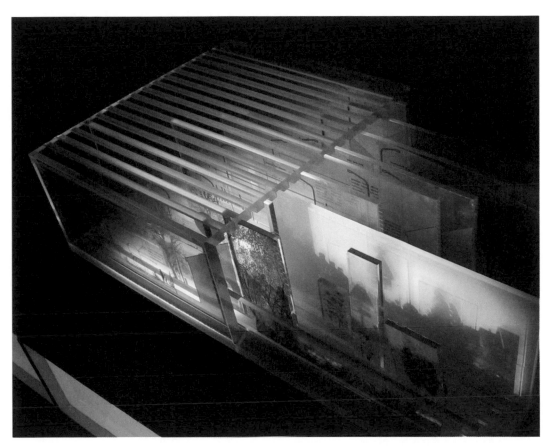

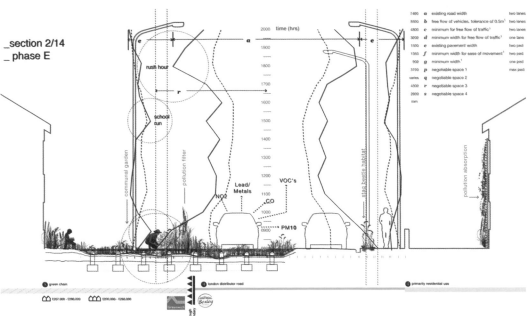

_section 2/14
_ phase E

Diploma Unit 15

*A polite notice to Mr Frampton,
some years later...*
The unit sites its explorations at the
historic intersection of species and
type as conjugated through context.
This year, our continued investigations
into typological adaptation to sites of
extreme political, economic and cultural
dimensions took us to the former
Panama Canal Zone and the peculiar
exigencies only such a geopolitical
anomaly could engender. In order to
allow the radical divergence of type it
required, we borrowed *character* from
Buffon and Adanson (the embedded
signature that serves to identify the
genus of even the most deviant
adaptations) to anchor typological
source. Perhaps not surprisingly, given
the special temporality of a country
defined by its status as a transit
economy through which everything
passes and nothing stays, time emerges
as a prime *material* in much of the work.
In the projects here, analysis of source
types, prison, factory and stock
exchange produce the characters'
institutionalisation, efficiency/
redundancy and waiting respectively.
Note in all three types the temporal is
already key.

Jean's market equates time with
organic waste. Scripted by the relative
shelf-life of fresh and preserved organic
waste, slow and fast 'compost glaciers'
transform the border landscape, erasing
a barrier yet to be disarmed in the
Panamanian psychogeography.

Sang Hoon sculpts from nightly fog,
global trade and the schedule of canal
transit a spatial and temporal site for a
futures exchange that diversifies the
canal's revenue.

Sang Yun's redundancy factory
fabricates a memorial landscape
scripted by the ghost history of abortive
works, sacrificed lives and submerged
towns, a veritable archaeology of
redundancy that underpins the
construction of the heroic canal.

In all, a hyper-contextuality to their
political, historic and economic sites
brings *context* firmly back into the fold –
that is they would not (could not) exist in
any other configuration of exigencies,
such is the stake-all-or-nothing
perversity of their critical specificity.
Looking back, Critical Regionalism
simply wasn't.

Unit Masters: Francesca Hughes,
Rita Lambert

Students: Sang Yun Kim, Heeseung Lee,
John Linares, Nicholas Lister,
Ed McCann, Sang Hoon Oh,
Toisin Oshinowo, Satpal Kaur Panesar,
Charles Peronin, Alan Smith,
Jean Chiying Wang

Technical Support: Matthew Wells,
Simon Beames

Jurors, Seminars and Workshops:
Noam Andrews, Shumon Basar, Artur
Carulla, Thomas Durner, Shin Egashira,
Homa Farjadi, Alex Haw, Christine
Hawley, Chris Lee, George L Legendre,
Tyen Masten, Martine de Maeseneer,
Hugh O'Shaunessy, Matthew Potter,
Stephen Roe, Brett Steele, Anne Save
de Beaurecueil, Charles Tashima,
Humberto Velez, Carlos Villanueva
Brandt, Mike Weinstock, Eyal Weizman

Special thanks to: Belinda Flaherty,
Antonia Loyd, Brett Steele, Mike
Weinstock and all the authorities
in Panama

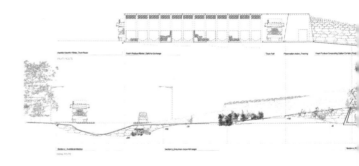

Jean Chiying Wang
*Shelf-Life:
The Preservation
and Decomposition
of a Political Border*

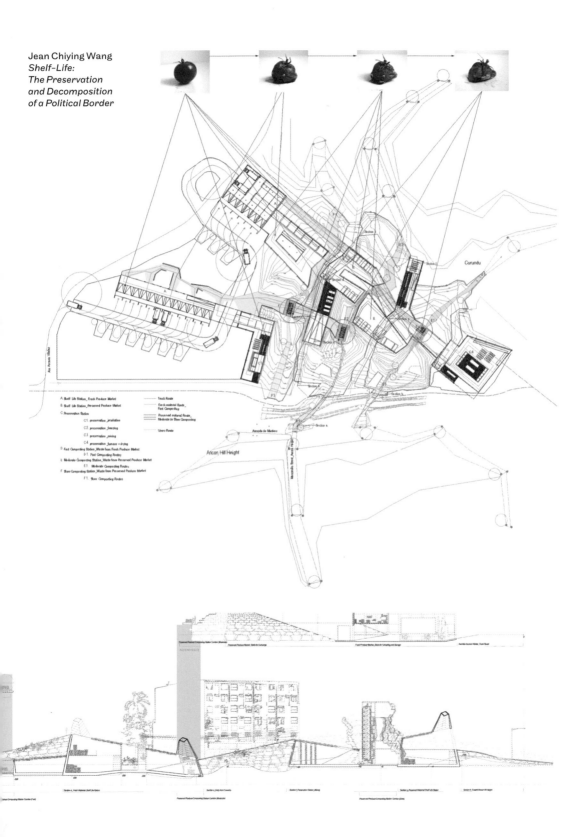

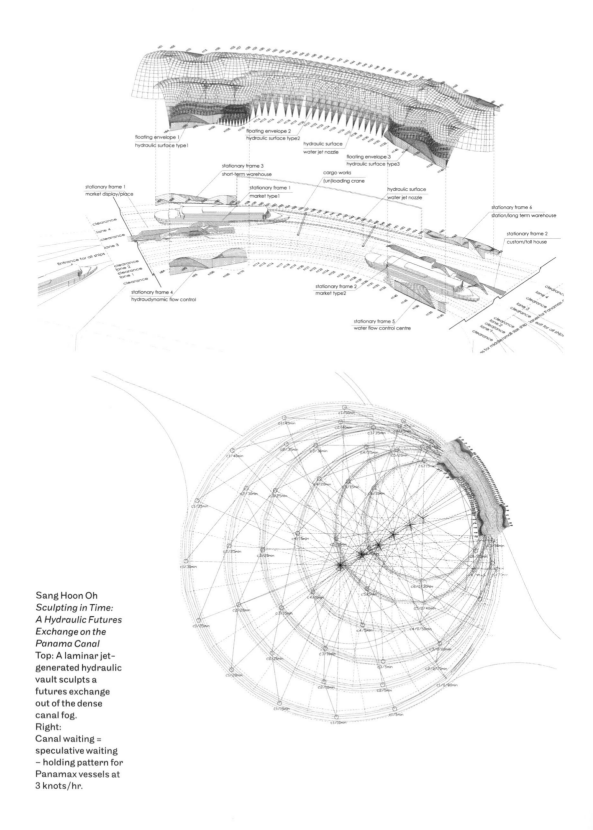

floating envelope 1
hydraulic surface type1

floating envelope 2
hydraulic surface type2

hydraulic surface
water jet nozzle

floating envelope 3
hydraulic surface type3

stationary frame 3
short-term warehouse

cargo works
(un)loading crane

hydraulic surface
water jet nozzle

stationary frame 1
market display/place

stationary frame 1
market type1

stationary frame 6
station/long term warehouse

stationary frame 2
custom/toll house

clearance
lane 4
clearance
lane 3
lane 3

Entrance for all ships

clearance
lane 2
clearance
lane 1
clearance

stationary frame 4
hydraudynamic flow control

stationary frame 2
market type2

stationary frame 5
water flow control centre

clearance
lane 4
clearance
lane 3
clearance
lane 2
clearance
lane 1
clearance

Sang Hoon Oh
*Sculpting in Time:
A Hydraulic Futures
Exchange on the
Panama Canal*
Top: A laminar jet-
generated hydraulic
vault sculpts a
futures exchange
out of the dense
canal fog.
Right:
Canal waiting =
speculative waiting
– holding pattern for
Panamax vessels at
3 knots/hr.

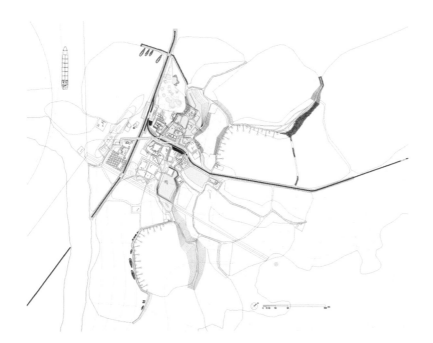

Sang Yun Kim
Redundant Histories: A Memorial Factory for the Panama Canal
Left: Negative islands: a memorial landscape for a ghost factory.
Below: Plotting the time and space of redundancy in the BMW Plant, Leipzig.

Diploma Unit 16

This year's research focuses on places that are exposed to extreme seismic activity and its consequences. Half a billion people live in close proximity to a volcano along the Pacific Rim and are affected by seismic activity and its aftermaths such as volcanic eruptions, earthquakes, landslides and tsunamis. In areas exposed to the hazard of natural disasters most funding tends to be invested in disaster relief. With pre-emptive design and mitigation strategies, much more could be done to reduce the effects of natural disasters on both lives and infrastructure.

We expect to demonstrate the importance of involving architects and other creative professionals who can assess the impact of natural disaster mitigation projects on the physical environment. These projects often represent a substantial financial, urbanistic and architectural investment, as well as an environmental one. Besides attempting to reduce the effects of a potential natural disaster they could also serve as incubators for the local and regional culture and economy and be an integral part of the built environment.

The research consists of an investigation into formal and material systems that could affect the behaviour of a natural system or phenomenon. In this exploration we are also aiming to develop simple rule-based conditions that allow for more complex and highly sophisticated systemic relationships to emerge between the form and the data/performance that informs it. The intention is to reach an understanding of some of the underlying effects of the built environment on the multi-layered complexity of the natural system or phenomenon control and vice versa.

Unit Masters: Steve Hardy,
Jonas Lundberg

Collaborator: Matti Lampila

Students: Itay Bachar, William Hai Liang Chen, Aidan Crawshaw, Abraham Gordon, Erik Brett Jacobsen, Kyu-Dong Jung, Kun-Wook Kang, Arthur Mamou-Mani, Dan Marks, Kauyhiro Murayama, Mina Papathanasiou, Jonathan Smith, Chun Chung Tong

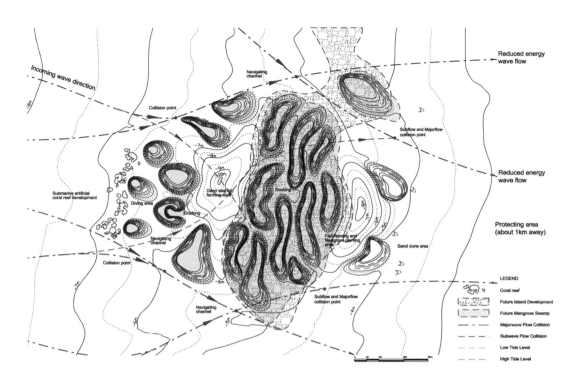

Natural barrier types   Proposal development

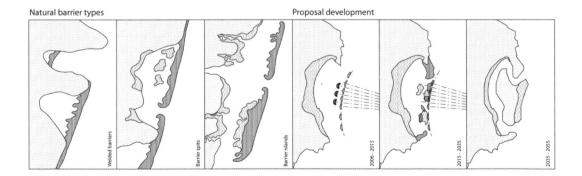

William Hai Liang Chen
Reef Surface Mobile Islands: Macro Scale
A zigzag series of mobile islands works as a breakwater, safeguarding the coastline and helping
to revive tourism. Mangrove tree planting underneath the spongy surface further dissipates wave
energy, while a fish farm is located in the wave-shadow zone. By embedding this artificial system
in the natural environment it is hoped to create a sustainable ecosystem stimulating the local
culture and economy.
Opposite page: Tsunami destruction, Sri Lanka, photo by Ashley de Vos (Galle Photographers)

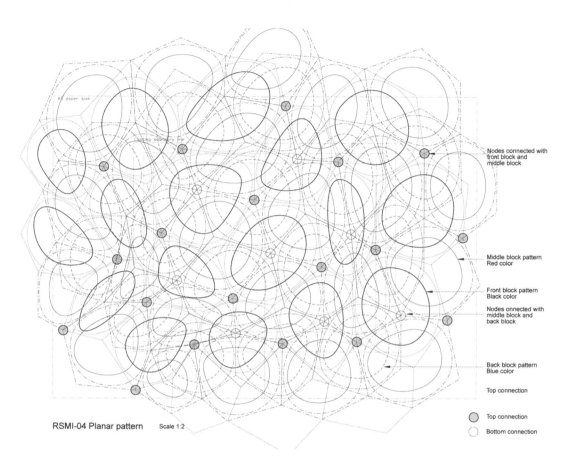

Nodes connected with
front block and
middle block

Middle block pattern
Red color

Front block pattern
Black color

Nodes onnected with
middle block and
back block

Back block pattern
Blue color

Top connection

⬤ Top connection

◯ Bottom connection

RSMI-04 Planar pattern   Scale 1:2

RSMI-01 Prototype   RSMI-01 Hydraulic performance

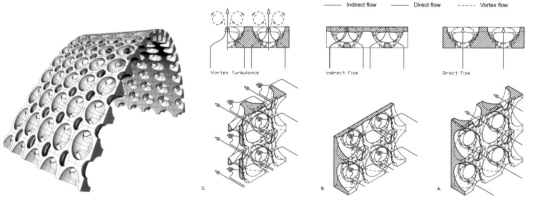

—— Indirect flow   —— Direct flow   ---- Vortex flow

Vortex Turbulence   indirect Flow   Direct Flow

C.   B.   A.

Reef Surface Mobile Islands: Micro Scale
A differentiated spongy surface as a type of breakwater armour
strengthens hydraulic stability and structural integrity performance.
Scale and porosity ratios will be specified according to location
(island to island) and wave–energy propagation.

RSMI-04 Plaster Casting Test

RSMI - 04 is aiming to produce a differentiated surface block morphology in order to achieve more structural rigidity and integrity. The geometry is generated from a differentiated 'zig-zag' arrangement of hexagonal and triangular typologies. In doing so this organisation produces a truss form in section. This structural orgamnisation holds similarity to that of mangrove's root structure.

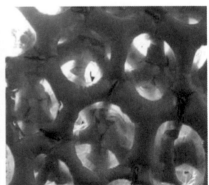

Material and Longevity
A variety of surface textures are essential for establishing marine life. Marine-friendly concrete will be developed for reef ball construction, while a de-inforced concrete solution will help the mangrove planting at the first stage, later breaking down into a seashell debris beach.

DRL Phase I Jury, June 2006
(photo Valerie Bennett)

Graduate School

AA Design Research Lab

The AA Design Research Lab [DRL] is a sixteen-month post-professional M(Arch) programme that differs in two fundamental ways from most graduate design settings. All design projects are pursued as collective proposals undertaken in small, self-organised teams addressing common topics through shared information-based diagrams, data, models and scripts. In addition, the DRL develops research agendas across three cycles of students, treating project-based design as a form of research and an engine for innovation.

For the last decade the DRL has continually explored the potentials of today's highly distributed, digital design networks and tools. The programme focuses on new forms of design thinking and skills needed to capture, control and shape an endless flow of information across these rapidly evolving design and production systems.

From 2002–05 the DRL worked on the design research agenda 'Responsive Environments', in which the relation of information to the distribution of matter guided the thesis proposals. In 2005–06, Phase 2 students completed the transition from Responsive Environments to Parametric Urbanism under the theme 'Create Space'. Briefs focused on the design of enhanced research environments for multidisciplinary work, urban infrastructures, and medical research and response schemes. Phase 1 students embarked on the development of the twenty-first century city where global connectivity is assumed. Urbanism can be understood to share characteristics of other complexities, including ecologies, environmental processes and artificial network organisations. Over the next three years, the studio will investigate the potential of new forms of intelligent, adaptive urbanism for sites in London at a critical time as the city undergoes its greatest expansion since the industrial revolution.

Staff: Yusuke Obuchi, Theodore Spyropoulos, Patrik Schumacher, Tom Verebes (Course Directors); Tom Barker, Christiane Fashek, Hanif Kara, Vasilis Stroumpakos

Phase 1 Students: Dmitris Akritopoulos, Andres Arias Madrid, Danilo Arsic, Lauren Barclay Thorne, Marc Boles, Kristof Crolla, Dominiki Dadatsi, Brian Curtis Dale, Oznur Erboga, Paulo Ernesto Flores Romero, Giulia Foscari Widmann Rezzonico, Eirini Fountoulaki, Luis Edgardo Fraguada, Sylvia Georgiadou, Yoshimasa Hagiwara, Gerard Thomas Filart Joson, Nantapon Jungurn, Mihee Kim, Kyungeun Kelly Lee, Sangyup Lee, Jose Luiz Lemos da Silva Neto, Shiqi Li, Lillie Liu, Arturo Lyon Gottlieb, Deniz Manisali, Theodora Ntatsopoulou, Iannis Orfanos, Victor Manuel Orive Garcia, Annarita Papeschi, Eleni Pavlidou, Karthikeyan Ramamoorthy, Jose Arturo Revilla Perez, Hala Sheikh, Sara Sheikh Akbari, Xiao Wei Tong, Jose Ramon Tramoyeres Rovira, Chrysostomos Tsimourdagkas, Ezhil Vigneswaran Ramaraju, Shih-Chin Wu, Shu-Hao Wu, Pavlos Xanthopoulos, Feng Xu

Phase 2 Students: Bassam Al Shiekh, Melike Altinisik, Ibraheem Ammash, Jimena Araiza, Maria Araya, Andrea Balducci, Ivan Ballesteros, Yevgeniy Beylkin, Shajay Bhooshan, Samer Chamoun, Jasmindar Chima, Ana Cocho, Carine Cohen, Florian Dubiel, Elif Erdine, Maria Loreto Flores, Elena Garcia, Amit Gupta, Khuzema Hussain, Amornchai Jaturawit, Nuruddin Karim, Muthahar Khan, Britta Knobel, Eugene Leung, Dao De Li, Stella Nikolakaki, Izwan Nor Azhar, Kaoruko Ogawa, Edgar Payan, Adam Pollonais, Arnoldo Rabago, Ahmad Sukkar, Margarita Valova, James Warton, Daniel Widrig, Sevil Yazici, Chang-Ki Yun, Xiaoyi Zhang

Top: DRL Phase 1 interim reviews, John Street Studios.
Bottom: 'Create Space', AA end-of-year exhibition July 2005.

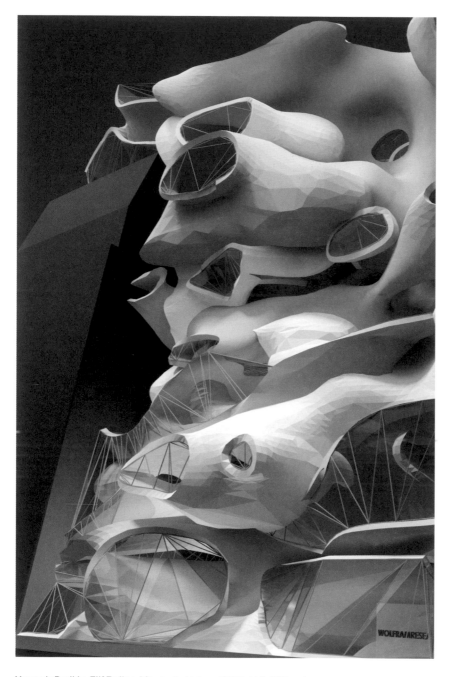

Yevgeniy Beylkin, Elif Erdine, Margarita Valova: *YME's Hybrid Species*
Phase 2 Thesis Studio, Brief: The Cellular Studio, Tutor: Brett Steele
YME's Hybrid Species rethinks the office building type by reflecting on the boundary condition
between two distinct organisations coexisting within an office block of London's financial district.
It employs a mathematical approach for developing complex spatial relationship. Mathematical
objects such as surfaces are divided into species each sharing a distinctive topology or equation,
utilising Triply Periodic Minimal Level Surfaces and Mathematica software to calculate and
visualise the topological transformations between species creating new hybrid surface topologies.

Opposite: Hybrid Species street level exterior view.
Top: Hybrid Species infills urban voids.
Above left: Lobby view of topological transformations.
Above right: Homotopic surfaces in section.

g_nome's NET.LAB: *Ibraheem Ammash, Jimena Araiza, Maria Loreto Flores, Ahmad Sukkar*
Phase 2 Thesis Studio, Brief: Skylab, Tutor: Tom Verebes
g_nome's research focused on proto-spatial production via evolutionary sequences of
algorithmic procedures to articulate social systems, scales and criteria. NET.LAB proposes a
fully distributed peer-to-peer architecture which attempts to connect different clients' working-
patterns as a non-linear Network Environment based on the Voronoi Diagram's algorithm. As a
design tool, the Voronoi Diagram does not separate walls, floors and structure, but blends them
in a volumetric whole.

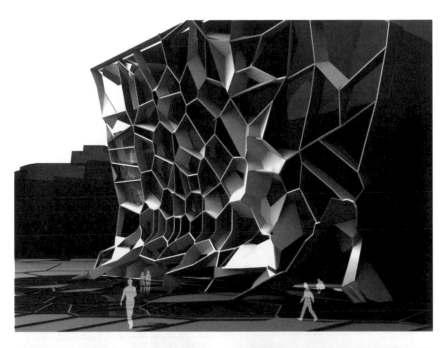

Opposite: Exterior view from London Metropolitan's square.
Top: Exterior view of Voronoi as structure in existing context.
Above left: Interior view of circulation and work space.
Above right: Skin experiments and lighting analysis.

Emerged's Hairs at Work: Melike Altinisik, Samer Chamoun, Daniel Widrig
Phase 2 Thesis Studio, Brief: Urban Lobby, Tutor: Patrik Schumacher
Emerged investigates the potential of fuzzy logic as a loose-fit organisational technique for developing intelligent, flexible and adaptive environments. The urban lobby is a continually contested and negotiated transient space; through it, the team explored ideas of form-finding and self-organisation on the site of Centrepoint. The project generates architectural interventions based on an understanding of the city as a dynamic field. The primary concerns are infrastructure as architecture, its impact on the confined site and its immediate adjacencies.

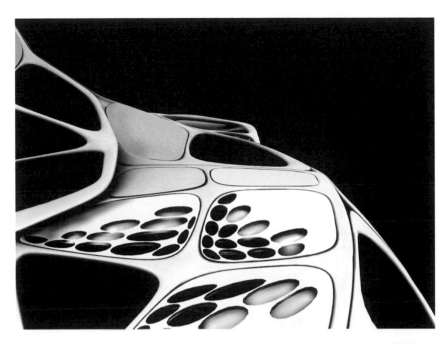

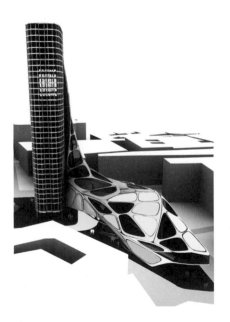

Opposite: Aerial view of the Hairs at Work connection to Centrepoint
Top: Close-up of exterior skin
Above left: View of proposed intervention at Centrepoint intersection
Above right: Interior view of Urban Lobby

Emergent Technologies and Design

Learning from Living Nature

This year the Emergent Technologies programme introduced a new module titled 'Nested Form-finding', an advance on more traditional methods for multiple hierarchy and multiple criteria form-finding. The seminar and studio module 'Natural Structures – Modelling and Analysis' received greater emphasis than in previous years. The programme organised numerous symposia and workshops that focused on biomimetic design strategies, advanced digital modelling, computer-aided manufacturing and computer-aided engineering.

Some recent work from the unit has been published in *Techniques and Technologies in Morphogenetic Design*, eds. Michael Hensel, Achim Menges and Michael Weinstock, AD Wiley, London 2006 and in *Emergence: Evolutionary Design Strategies*, eds. Michael Hensel, Achim Menges and Michael Weinstock, AD Wiley, London 2004. See also aaschool.ac.uk/et.

From the beginning of the next academic year in October EmTech will offer a 12-month MSc degree as an addition to its accredited degree programme.

EmTech congratulates its graduate Juan Eduardo Subercaseaux, who received his MArch with Distinction.

Staff: Michael Hensel, Michael Weinstock (Directors); Achim Menges (Studio Master); Martin Hemberg, Prof George Jeronimidis (Visiting Staff)

External Examiners: Prof Tony Atkins, Prof Chris Wise

Phase 02 2005/06 Students: Guillem Baraut, Jennifer DeGaetano Boheim, Janice Chiu, Ioannis Douridas, Mattia Gambardella, Pavel Hladik, Joshua Mason, Premveer Nagpal, Kathleen O'Donnell, Emerson Porras, Jonathan Rabagliati, Veerapatt Teeravutichai, Chen Ying-Tsai, Taek Yong Yoon

MA 2005: Efrat Cohen, Michel Da Costa Gonçalves, Biraj Rajan Ruvala, Zoe Saric Kelez, Atul Singla, Thomas von Girsewald, Li Zou

MArch 2006: Juan Eduardo Subercaseaux (with Distinction)

EmTech would like to thank:
Daniel Coll I Capdevila, Prof Julian Vincent, Simos Yannas
Buro Happold: Mike Cook, Jalal El-Ali, Lawrence Friesen, Nikolaos Stathopoulos, Wolf Mangelsdorf
Bentley Systems and the Smart Geometry Group: Robert Aish, Francis Aish, Kaustuv DeBiswas, Lars Hasselgren, Roly Hudson, Axel Kilian, Hugh Whitehead, Prof Chris Williams, Rob Woodbury

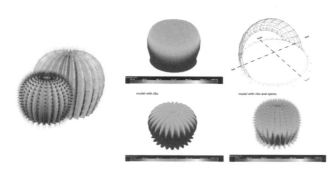

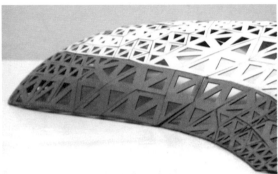

View of north facade of the envelope from the east   Detail of differntiated surface

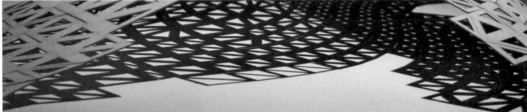

Partial viewfrom the outside of unfinished envelope and light pattern at floor level.

Diferentiated light pattern at the inside of the building floor level

Light modulated by envelope projected at floor level (building interior). Difuse borders.

Sunlight Pattern
Observation of surface details and light patterns

These images show the behaviour of light as it passes through the envelope, indicating the overall decrease in the amount of light and the clear effect that the different components on the surface level have on the light patterns inside. Looking at the shadow patterns at floor level, we can see how the borders between permeability zones are located at the surface. The difference between the light qualities at surface level on the outside of the building (strong contrasted light) and the light quality in the interior (more smooth and even with diffuse borders) can also be observed.

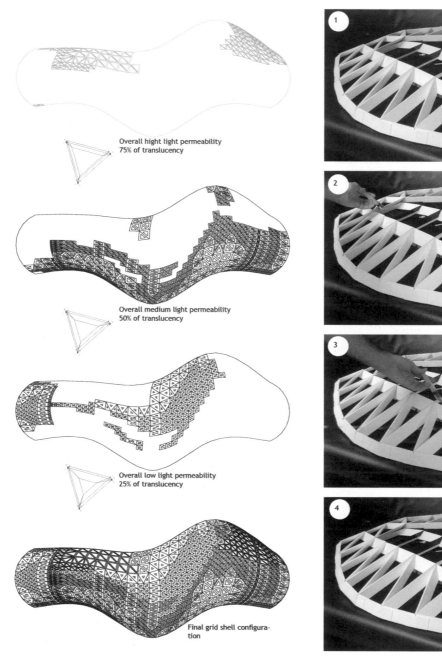

Overall hight light permeability
75% of translucency

Overall medium light permeability
50% of translucency

Overall low light permeability
25% of translucency

Final grid shell configuration

Population Logic: Population procedure defined by light exposure throughout the year. The light permeability strategy defined for the building will set the population logic, defining the degree of transparency of each of the components to be nested in the tessellation layout. The images show the specific zoning of the three kinds of components through the surface, in relation to their translucency level. The image at the bottom shows the final configuration of the building with the three zones combined.

Analogue model: Activation sequence
The articulated part of the middle hangs in a relaxed manner leaving gaps between its sides and the locked frame. As the pneumatic devices are stimulated, the articulated part achieves curvature and the gaps get closed. Thus the structure switches from a permeable to a sealed one.

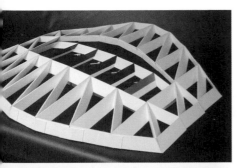

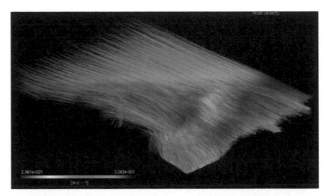

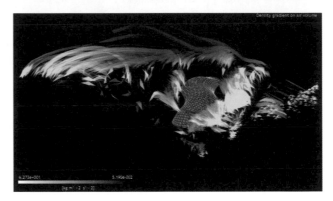

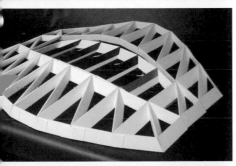

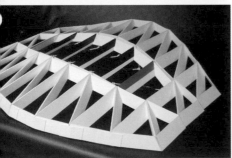

CFD: Wind flow affected by building and surrounding environment. Wind velocity and density gradient on air volume. In the image at the top, the influx zone is at the right hand side, the green colour symbolises the original wind speed, set at 10m/s according to the site meteorological records for springtime. The red zones of the image describe an increase in wind velocity. Because of the shape of the envelope designed, the wind flow is accelerated through the surface achieving the highest speed at the top of the surface – red zones – defining there the low pressure zones. Because of the smooth wing-like shape of the envelope, the increase and decrease of the speed is gradual, going from greens to reds and back to greens.
The image at the bottom shows the density gradient of the air volume around the building and surrounding site. Since the increase of density can be translated into decrease of speed, this graph corroborates the ability of the building to control wind flow, as no increase of density is shown directly over the building. Instead, it is directly above the square volumes around the building.

Histories & Theories

The Histories & Theories programme is designed to provide students with a critical understanding of contemporary architecture and debates. We believe this is best achieved through an emphasis on architecture as the outcome of knowledge of histories and forms of practice. Central to the courses is the investigation and critical reassessment of twentieth-century architecture and urbanism, in terms of formal analysis and spatial organisation and the different theories that engage with them.

The programme attracts a wide variety of students, this year from Ecuador, Germany, Greece, Japan, Israel, Portugal, South Korea, Spain and New Zealand. Whereas the majority were architects wishing to spend a year to reflect upon some of the theoretical implications of their design practice or take the first steps in an academic career, three students, from interior design, art and engineering, participated in the programme in order to acquire an understanding of architectural theory and its relation to particular projects.

In addition to attending lectures and participating in an open theory seminar series with visiting theorists, architects and critics, students were encouraged to take full advantage of other events in the School, including an active engagement in this year's research clusters. This year's trip, to Como, Italy, and the establishing of links with the Foundation Terragni and the Polytechnic School in Milan, offered students a unique opportunity to study the work of Giuseppe Terragni.

Visiting Theory Seminars 2005/06

Robert Somol, 'Whatever Happened to Picking Fights?', November 2005
In the first of two visits to the AA this year, Ohio State University Baumer Visiting Professor Bob Somol made the case that, 'A fully projective practice will have to move off the faith in social or techno-sciences that an exotic site or a new technology appears to provide. Architecture isn't rocket (or any other) science. It's just politics.'

Sarah Whiting, 'Architecture's Social Imaginary', January 2006
In addition to her Evening Lecture, 'Looking Good', Whiting gave two open theory seminars, all of which reconsidered architecture's formalist legacy in an effort to situate the discussion within the contemporary public sphere. Among the central questions she sought to answer were: 'How do we evaluate, judge, talk about, and advance architecture?' 'Who's looking our way and how?' 'Who are we looking for and why?'

Cynthia Davidson, 'An Introduction to *Log*: Observations on Architecture and the Contemporary City', January 2006
Davidson, editor of *Log*, presented the journal's 'project' and the ways in which articles in its early editions have engaged architecture and the city and related cultural issues.

Anthony Vidler, 'Histories of the Immediate Present', February 2006
Tony Vidler, architectural historian and Dean of the Cooper Union, returned to the AA to discuss topics in his books *The Architectural Uncanny*, *Warped Space* and the forthcoming *Histories of the Immediate Past*, a sort of intellectual biography of the four figures central to his development as an architectural historian.

Michael Speaks, 'Design Intelligence: Thinking in Architecture After the End of Theory', March 2006
In the first of his two seminars, Speaks focused on the rise and fall of architecture theory-vanguardism and the influence of Derrida and Deleuze, tracking two very different possibilities for 'architectural thinking after the end of metaphysics'. His second seminar looked at an emergent form of 'architectural thinking' or design intelligence evident in the work of a new generation of practitioners who are

more concerned with the 'plausible truths' generated through prototyping and scenario development than with the 'received truths' of theory or philosophy.

Staff: Mark Cousins (Director), Katharina Borsi, Marina Lathouri, Robert Maxwell

Visiting Lecturers: Aristidis Antonas, Pier Vittorio Aureli, Andrew Benjamin, Kathrin Böhm and Andreas Lang, Cynthia Davidson, Christiane Fashek, George L Legendre, Robert Somol, Michael Speaks, Anthony Vidler, Sarah Whiting

Students: Eleni Axioti, Tal Bar, Marc Britz, Yoko Fukada, Seungmin Kang, José Maria Monfá Guix, Lisette Keats, Christina Papadimitriou, Christian Parreno, Ana Rute Faisca, Telemachos Telemachou, Kirk Wooller

2005/06 Thesis Submisssions

Eleni Axioti
Architecture as Destruction

Tal Bar
The Role of the Skyscraper in a Changing Urban Environment

Marc Britz
New York Short Circuits: Ungers, Koolhaas, Tschumi and the City

Yoko Fukada
The Regeneration of the Naoshima Island

Seungmin Kang
The Contemporary South Korean Dwelling and City: Transfer and Appropriation of Traditional Tools and Processes

Lisette Keats
Neutra and the Therapeutic Intention

Jose Maria Monfa Guix
Building Effects

Christina Papadimitriou
An 'Ancient' Landscape: The Case of the Athenian Acropolis

Christian Parreno
Operations of the Formless in Contemporary Architecture

Ana Rute Faisca
Copy and Paste: How to Turn a Dutch House into a Portuguese Concert Hall in Under Two Weeks

Telemachos Telemachou
Reading Urban Complexity: Public and Private

Kirk Wooller
Figuring Nothing Out: The Politics of Architectural Form in the Contemporary City

Housing & Urbanism

The Housing & Urbanism programme
is concerned with the interplay of
urbanism as a spatial discipline and the
political processes of the city. This is
studied through the critique of the main
understandings and practices in
urbanism, and through experimentation
with alternative methods and tools of
spatial design. The MA course is
structured around three primary types
of student work: design workshops,
which investigate urban areas and test
design strategies in a real context;
lectures and seminars, exploring
theoretical and critical issues related to
the concepts and approaches developed
in the design work; and thesis work,
through which students develop an
extended study within the field.

Within the programme three lines of
investigation, consultancy and funded
research are being developed which
both expose the limitations of prevailing
practices in urbanism and urban design
and call for alternative approaches:
– Investigating the role of urbanism in
enhancing 'innovation environments'
and 'knowledge-based' clusters through
their urbanisation – in contrast to earlier
models of science and technology parks.
– Exploring what is an appropriate
urbanism to address urban irregularity
and informality and to engage with the
interaction of spatial strategies and
urban social policies.
– Developing a critical reasoning
about housing densities and urban
intensification, in which architecture is
seen more dynamically in relation to an
urban process.

The design workshops in London,
Shanghai and Bilbao explored these
themes in real project situations,
collaborating with the relevant
stakeholders in a quasi consultancy
format.

Courses
Design workshops, terms 1 & 2
Cities in a transnational world, term 1
The reason of urbanism, term 1
Critical urbanism, terms 1 & 2
Housing and the irregular city, term 2
Shaping the modern city, term 2
Domesticity, term 2

Staff: Jorge Fiori, Lawrence Barth,
Nicholas Bullock, Hugo Hinsley,
Dominic Papa, Elena Pascolo,
Carlos Villanueva Brandt
Teaching assistants: Tarsha Finney,
Pavlos Philippou

Students: Stephen Bamonte,
Renata Bertol Domingues, Juan Oriol
Busquets Vila, Li-Chun Chang, Aida
Esteban Millat, Mattia Gambardella,
Abraham Jimenez Ovando, Yee Tak Lau,
Chang Min Lee, Julissa Lopez-Hodoyan,
Jing Lu, Aristeidis Makris, Fernando
Poucell Mier y Teran, Luis Salazar
Machado, Marco Sanchez Castro,
Sophia Tseliou, Daniela Uribe Saieg,
Tiberio Wallentin, Jeremy Zuidema

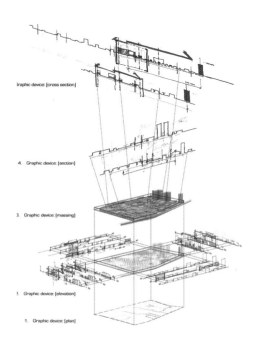

Graphic device: [cross section]

4. Graphic device: [section]

3. Graphic device: [massing]

2. Graphic device: [elevation]

1. Graphic device: [plan]

Shanghai Workshop
A joint workshop with the College of Architecture and Planning at Tongji University is exploring the concept of an urbanised innovation environment in relation to existing medical and research facilities in Fenglin. Left: Dislocating boundaries to configure. Top: Biomedical network – from local to urban scale. Above: Study block – exploring options.

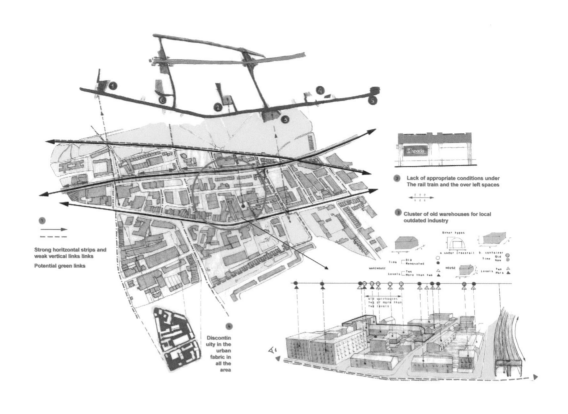

FORMAL LIMITS   APPROPIATION   FLOODING

Hackney Workshop
Hackney lies midway between the consolidated centre of London and the rapidly changing zone to the east that runs
from Stratford City to the Lea Valley with the 270-hectare Olympics site. We developed proposals for part of central
Hackney, where the physical fabric is heterogeneous and disrupted, with a wide range of scales and types of buildings
and spaces. Top: Spatial and infrastructural movement. Above: Testing the negotiation ground of unbuilt spaces.
Opposite page, top: Brake spaces – configuring the urban district. Opposite page, bottom: Permeable urban fabric.

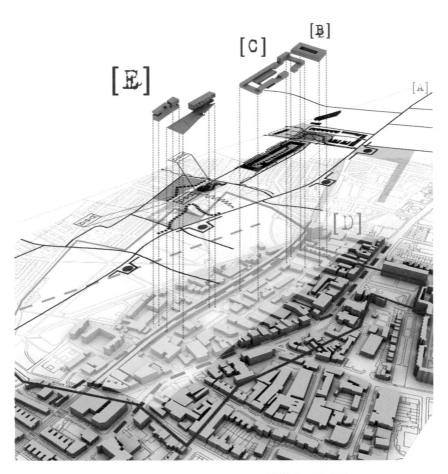

Testing Typologies In the Deep Block

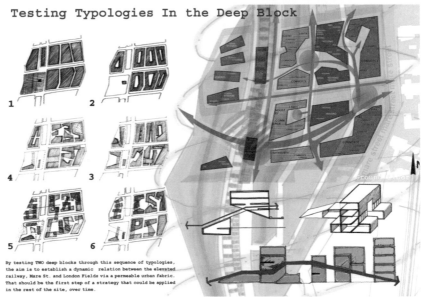

By testing TWO deep blocks through this sequence of typologies,
the aim is to establish a dynamic relation between the elevated
railway, Mare St. and London Fields via a permeable urban fabric.
That should be the first step of a strategy that could be applied
in the rest of the site, over time.

Landscape Urbanism

The AA Graduate School's Landscape Urbanism programme is a twelve-month studio-based course designed for students who are interested in integrating, within the domain of urbanism, the techniques and modes of operation historically described as landscape design. The programme's aim is to open up fields of exploration that move fluidly across disciplinary boundaries, in an attempt to develop inclusive paradigms and modes of practice which are able to transform broad territories, and to affect the organisation and coordination of complex systems.

The programme is structured around a full-time design studio in which students confront projects of increasing complexity and develop techniques and innovative design solutions. This year the focus was on Sri Lanka, following the devastation of the tsunami. In planning for the reconstruction and reoccupation of these areas, it is important to identify potential hazard zones so as to avoid future loss of life and property. At the same time, the new socio-political con-figurations that arose as an immediate consequence of the local death toll call for a reinterpretation of traditional patterns of spatial inhabitation, at both macro and micro scales.

The four terms of study are divided into two phases. The topics and objectives that serve as the programme's focus are introduced and elaborated in design studio projects, seminars and workshops during the first phase. Design Studio courses are pursued through all three terms of this phase. Workshops and seminars held during terms 1 and 2 expose students to a wide range of contemporary landscape theories and techniques, and introduce seminal projects. During the second phase – covering the summer period – students complete a comprehensive individual design thesis project which demonstrates the skills and knowledge acquired in the first three terms.

Staff: Eva Castro, Leyre Asensio Villoria, David Mah, Eduardo Rico (Design Studio), Sandra Morris, Larry Barth, Ian Carradice + Arup (Seminars)

Lectures and Workshops: Dillon Lin, Roly Hudson, Marco Poletto, Ivan Valdez

Students: Eduardo Carranza, Min Hsiang Chen, Moojan Kalbasi, Elena Kanakoudi, Io Karydi, Athina Kokla, Carolina Lopez, Sang Hyeok Lee, Bridget MacKean, Leo Ng Keok Poh, Manuel Schmidt, Zoe Spiegel, Christabel Lee Hoi Ting, Chimin Yang

Guest Critics: Arjan Scheer, Chris Lee, Claudia Pasquero, Dyfed Autrey, Friedrich Ludewig, Gabriel Duarte, Gunter Gassner, Irénée Scalbert, Ivan Valdez, James Khamsi, Jeff Turko, John Skelly, Jose María Aguirre Aldaz, Katharina Borsi, Katka Schaffer, Marco Poletto, L.H. Idrasiri, Prasanna Silva, Roly Hudson, Samitha Manawadn, Varuna da Silva, Brett Steele, Karola Dierichs, Anthony Peter

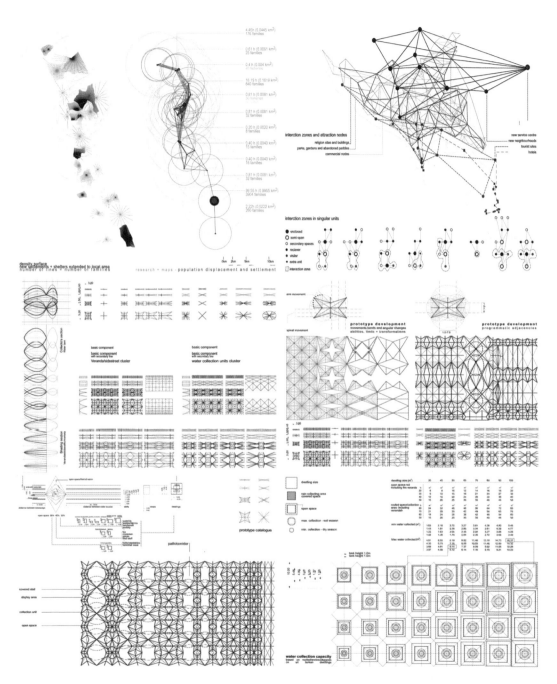

Moojan Kalbasi
Vaulted Landscapers, Galle, Sri Lanka
Galle has the potential to be developed as a tourist town, though its fine streetgrain has suffered many years of neglect.
Inspired by the old verandas and courtyards traditionally used as zones of interaction, this project focuses on creating
north–south corridors of veranda streets and market squares through the development of a prototype system which
hybridises the structures of vaulted markets, souks, arched verandas and domestic rain water harvesting. The design
aims to draw tourism into the heart of the city neighbourhoods and to reinstate the fine streetgrain for social interaction.
Overleaf: Site proliferation and fabric detail

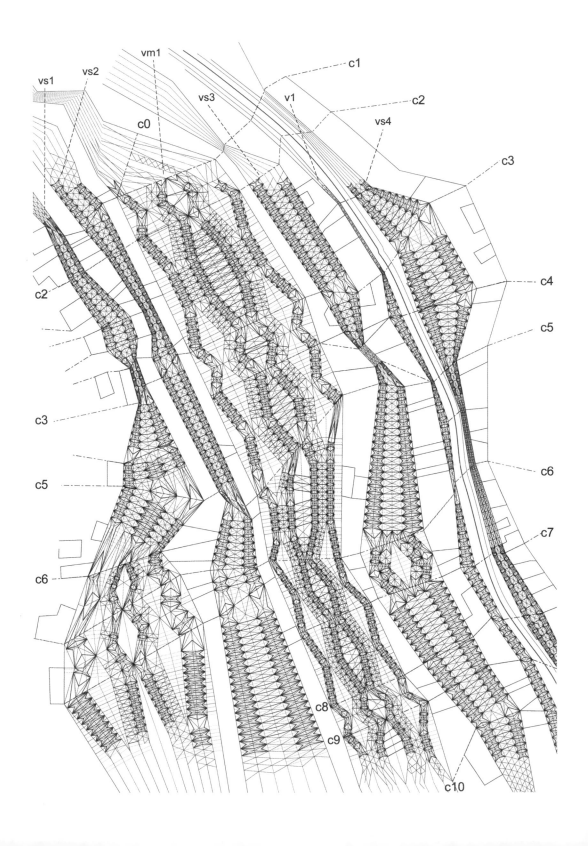

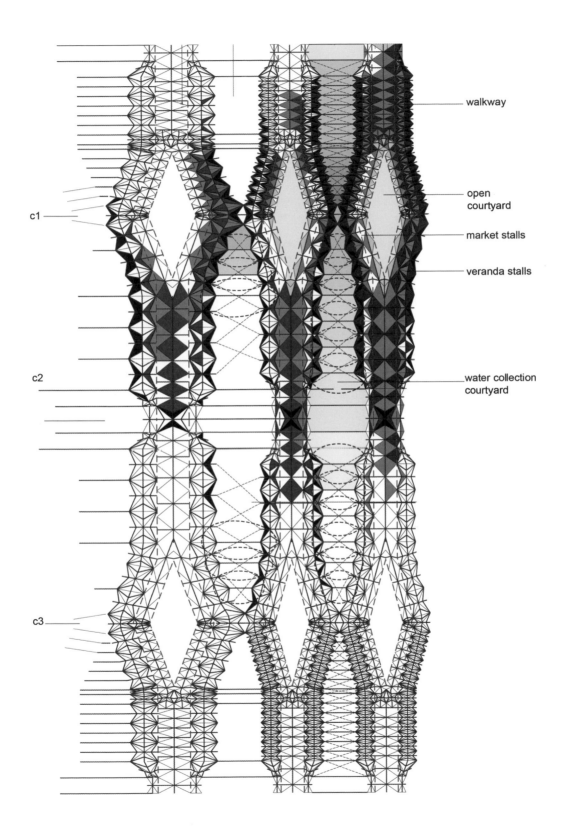

walkway

open
courtyard

market stalls

veranda stalls

c1

c2

water collection
courtyard

c3

Sustainable Environmental Design

This is the first year of the 12-month MSc and 16-month MArch in Sustainable Environmental Design, which replaced the MA in Environment & Energy Studies. The main research object of both MSc and MArch is the relationship between architectural form, materiality and environmental performance and how this relationship is affected by climate, building programme and operational parameters. This year the MSc and MArch shared the same taught content of lectures and software workshops and worked on the same project briefs. First and second term projects were undertaken in teams of three students.

The year started with a one-week project to redesign a commercial building in Athens. This was followed by fieldwork to study daylighting in art galleries in London and a short project using the knowledge gained to design an exhibition space. The second term was devoted to a single project on the design of learning environments. Dissertation projects were started in May and are still at early research stages. These are undertaken individually and cover a wide range of topics. The first MSc students will graduate at the end of September 2006, the first MArch in January 2007.

Staff: Simos Yannas, Klaus Bode, Werner Gaiser, Raul Moura, Peter Sharratt

Students: Ahmed Aly Abouzeid, Tobi Adamolekun, Giles Bruce, Haven Burkee, Joyce Chan, Anastasia Dreta, Clarice Fong, Manuel Alejandro Gallardo, Chanin Kemakawat, Varun Kohli, Natalia Kokosalaki, Sayed Zabihullah Majidi, Federico Montella, Debra Raymont, Vasiliki Sagia, Aadil Salim, Sandro Tubertini, Olga Tzioti, Steven Vujeva, Chi-Tsun Wang

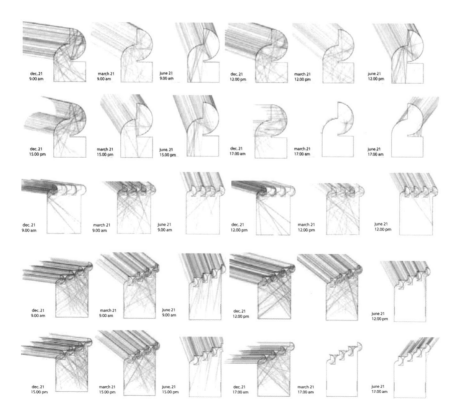

Sayed Zabihullah Majidi (this page) and Giles Bruce (opposite page), alternative roof variants for Sackler Galleries, Royal Academy, London, following from team project on existing lighting conditions in the exhibition spaces.

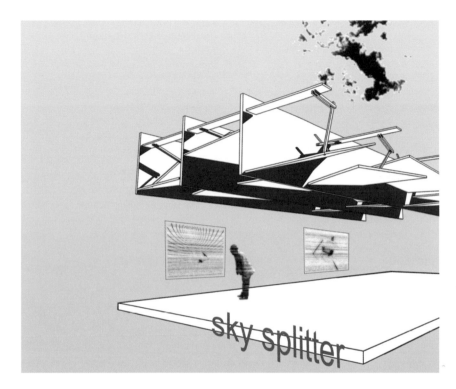

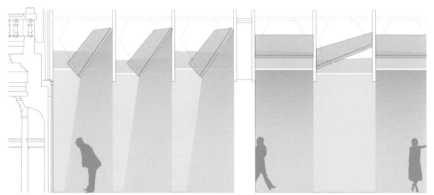

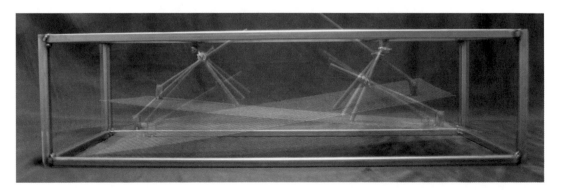

Haven Burkee, Natalia Kokosalaki, Sayed Zabihullah Majidi
Proposals for a multifunctional canopy for a nineteenth-century school building in London

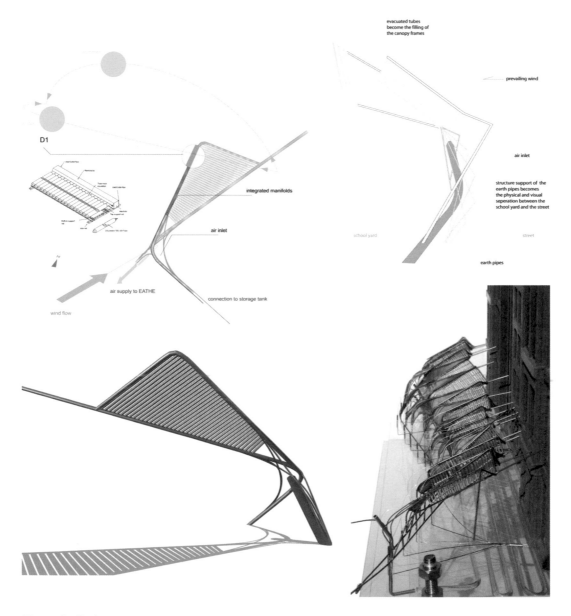

Dissertation Projects
Ahmed Aly Abouzeid *The Sustainable Urban* Tobi Adamolekun *Open System Construction for Self-Build Housing in Lagos* Giles Bruce (MArch) *Energy Efficient Apartments for Ireland's Atlantic Coastline* Haven Burkee (MArch) *Passive Cooling for Residential Design in the Florida Keys* Jay Chan *Public 'Living-Room' in Hong Kong* Anastasia Dreta *Office Buildings in Mediterranean Climate* Clarice Fong *Adaptive Reuse of Industrial Buildings* Alejandro Gallardo Gonzalez *Prototype House for Small-Scale Development in Baja Sur, Mexico* Chanin Kemakawat *Bangkok Row Houses* Varun Kohli *Creating Learning Environments in Nilgiri Hills,*

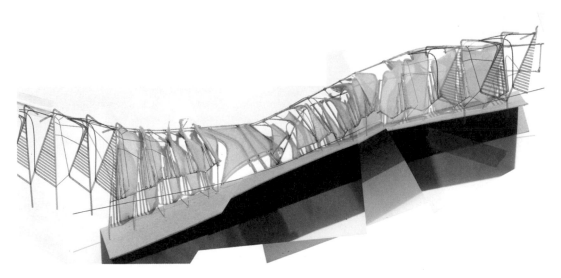

Southern India Natalia Kokosalaki (MArch) *Following the Olympic Games in Athens: Redesigning and Reuse* Sayed Zabihullah Majidi (MArch) *A Housing Strategy for the Periphery of Kabul City* Federico Montella *Environmental Functions of a Buffer Space for a Commercial Building* Debra Raymont *Low Income Housing through Sustainable Design* Vasiliki Sagia *Design of Commercial Building in Athens* Aadil Salim *Adapting the Courtyard in Warm-Humid Climates* Sandro Tubertini *Office Building in Sao Paulo* Olga Tzioti *A Contemporary Academic Library in Athens* Steven Vujeva *Sustainable Alterations to Long Island Dwellings* Chi-Tsun Wang *Environmental Attributes of Bamboo Houses in Warm-Humid Regions*

Building Conservation

This year's work developed awareness and skills in the core subjects of Historic Knowledge and Cultural Appreciation; Research and Report Writing; Philosophy of Conservation; Traditional Building Materials; Structures of Historic Buildings; Fabric Deterioration and Repair; Building Investigations, Inspections and Assessments; and Conservation and Design in Modern Urban Contexts.

In addition to developing a wide range of knowledge concerning historic buildings of all periods, the programme increasingly emphasises twentieth-century buildings and environs, along with the current political and social issues of urban redevelopment, change and sustainability.

Lectures are reinforced by visits to current projects or to locations reflecting current issues. There were also two weekend study tours, the first investigating churches and the second medieval domestic buildings and castles.

Visits to workshops and studios have included CEL, Peterborough – Lead Casting; Hampton Court Palace – Brick Repair Workshops; the AA – Lime Workshop; Salisbury Cathedral Workshops – Stonemasons Yard; Bulmer's Brickworks, Suffolk – Traditional Brick Manufacture.

The end of year visit was to the recently repaired and conserved Moggerhanger House at Sandy in Bedfordshire, an important design by Sir John Soane. We then visited the 1920s airship sheds at Cardington, home to the ill-fated R101, and Woburn Abbey to see how a major estate is managed and how its buildings are maintained and used. We discussed the issues of nearby urban and airport expansion and how these affect the character of historic buildings and landscapes, including the introduction of lions and giraffes into the English landscape.

Staff: John Redmill (Director), Alan Greening (Master), Andrew Shepherd (Tutor), Sue Blundell (Thesis tutor), Clement Chung (Co-ordinator)

Visiting Lecturers: Ian Bristow, Sharon Cather, Bridget Cherry, Stephen Clare, Kate Clark, Alan Frost, Adrian Gibson, Diane Green, Richard Halsey, Julian Harrap, Richard Harris, Jacques Heyman, Rosemary McQueen, Tim Palmer, Sam Price, Clive Richardson, Eric Robinson, Sarah Stainforth, Robert Thorne, Roger White, Tony Walker

First Year Students: Colin Brooking, Nerida Campbell, Louise Dandy, Katharine De Haan, Dianna Floud, Mary Nee, Stephen Parris, Jacqueline Pope, William Reading

Second Year Students/Thesis submissions;
Viorica Feler-Morgan *Jerusalem 1920s and 1930s International Style in Architecture – Rehavia neighbourhood* Harriet Harriss *Powerhouse – The Power of Politics, Process and Participation in the Conservation Strategies of London Power Stations* David Hills *BARBICAN: MODern CONServation?* David Jackson *The Conservation and Management of Monuments in Developing Countries – with particular reference to Lalibela, Ethiopia* Anna Joynt *Old Havana: Restoration and Utopia* Ellen Leslie *Ice Houses of Greater London* Mark Pearce *The Development of the Ecclesiastical Architecture of Sharpe, Paley and Austin* Miriam Volic *Maxwell Fry's Fine Buildings* Wyndham Westerdale *Pavilions of Pleasure: The Banqueting House in Sixteenth- and Seventeenth-Century England*

Joint end-of-year visit, Danson House, Bexleyheath, Kent

Landscape Conservation & Change

Characteristic territories and designed landscapes are among the most precious inheritances that countries have. Whilst landscapes need to be cared for, perhaps restored, they also sometimes need to be laid out afresh in order to meet contemporary require-ments and aspirations, thus introducing new values.

Now in its final year, the AA Graduate School's Landscape Conservation & Change programme has attuned over 200 students to these issues over 20 years. It has taken a progressive approach, centred around the choices to be made in resolving the dilemmas of a living record of past human achievements and associations that must also be the venue for fresh successes that overlay the old.

The English landscape and its parks and gardens have been a particular source of inspiration to generations of artists, writers and designers, and English practice in landscape conservation is renowned world-wide. On the other hand, the programme has also considered the subject from a wider international perspective.

While the programme has been designed to encourage thinking on broad issues, it has also introduced the tech-niques of research, analysis, evaluation, criticism, and management planning. But perhaps the best preparation for dealing with landscapes in an ever-changing world has been the develop-ment of personal philosophies and ethics that will ensure a principled approach to whatever complex and unpredictable issues arise.

These intellectual perspectives have been 'grounded' by examination of the consequences of past and recent decisions, and the responses they generated. Students have thereby been more able to think and act sympatheti-cally and competently with regard to the treatment of landscapes, from the initial survey to the final report or plan.

The course has attracted architects, landscape architects, town and country planners, garden historians and park managers, as well as the occasional art historian, lawyer and journalist. Students were often mid-career, and saw the programme as a chance to consider their future direction, or to engineer a career change. Others were recently qualified in their field, but felt that previous learning left them eager to advance their theoretical insights before embarking on their career. Yet others intended the MA as a step towards research in the future.

Staff: David Jacques, PhD, MSc, DipTP, MIHT, MRTPI (Programme Director and tutor for Change in Landscape and Futures), Axel Griesinger, Dipl.Ing, Grad Dip Cons Gardens (AA) (Form & Style tutor), Jan Woudstra, PhD, MACons, DipHort (Kew) (Historic Details tutor), Clement Chung (Co-ordinator)

Guest lecturers in recent years: Drew Bennellick, Andre Berry, Chris Blandford, Marion Blockley, Charles Boot, Paul Bramhill, Jane Brown, Jim Buckland, Nick Burton, Henry Cleere, Dominic Cole, Alessandra Como, Susan Denyer, Joy Ede, Brent Elliott, Benoit Fondu, John Glenn, Patrick Goode, Alan Greening, Nick Haycock, Alison Hems, Virginia Hinze, Richard Hughes, Jonathan Lovie, Ana Luengo, Amanda Mathews, John Phibbs, Jill Raggett, Judith Shaw, Chris Sumner, Michael Symes, Christopher Taylor, Hilary Taylor, Julia Thrift, Jennifer Ullman, Jenifer White, Kim Wilkie

MA Students/Dissertation submissions: Susan Brice, The State and Future of Designed Landscapes That Have Lost Their Houses, Caroline Grant Conservation of the Coastline in Britain and Western Australia
Diploma Students: Mary-Ann Baynes, Jennifer Howard, Ian Hussein, Helen Langley

Clockwise from top left: Blenheim Palace (photo Fred Scott), Chatsworth House (Sandra Morris), Rousham House (Laurence Webber), Chatsworth House (Andrew Holmes), Chatsworth House (Sandra Morris), Chatsworth House (Sandra Morris),

PhD Programme

The Joint Programme for PhD studies combines advanced research with a broader agenda preparing graduates for practice in global academic and professional environments. Currently in its second year, it encompasses research in the fields of architectural history and theory, architectural urbanism and sustainable environ-mental design. Nine new PhD research proposals are being put forward for registration this year and 27 projects continued from previous years are at various stages of development, with nearly half expected to complete within 2006. Four PhD seminars were offered, addressing specific requirements of the different research groups as well as broader issues of PhD research. PhD and MPhil research degrees at the AA are administered in partnership with the Open University's Research School.

Staff: Simos Yannas, Lawrence Barth, Nicholas Bullock, Mark Cousins, Jorge Fiori, Hugo Hinsley, Marina Lathouri, Peter Sharratt

Seminars

Architectural Urbanism
Lawrence Barth
Drawing upon Foucault's archaeological writings, this seminar investigated the relationship between themes and concepts in the field of architectural urbanism. This year its focus was the role of typology in urban strategy and transformation. The group worked con-sistently with two subtle but important divergences from most work in architec-tural urbanism: typology was viewed as a more dynamic domain of experimen-tation than usual, and the diagram was treated as having a greater degree of historical persistence. Together, these attitudes became part of a general remapping of the relation between architecture and an urban discursive formation. The perspective of the seminar aims to balance historical investigation and practical application.

Occidentalism
Mark Cousins
This research seminar sought to develop themes in current PhD projects related to contemporary Asian architecture and urbanism. It related to the other side of the coin of orientalism which concerns western fantasies about the East. The seminar looked at the way in which western architecture and urbanism is appreciated in Asia on grounds of modernisation, but turns out to have a different signification to that in the west.

Spatial Scales and Drawing Systems
Marina Lathouri
This research seminar sought to look at the ways in which forms of theoretical research in current PhD projects are related to design and modes of representation. The question of architectural representation and form was investigated through extended analyses of readings seeking to balance between historical investigation and current applications. Themes and techniques were further developed around the research areas of students interested in reviewing visual and graphic evidence primarily as tools of architectural and urban research.

Productive Research
Simos Yannas
It may not come as a surprise that in a field as varied as architecture is today there can be many different interpreta-tions of what constitutes research, how it should be undertaken and what may be worthy outcomes. In highlighting some of the differences this seminar provided a platform for discussion and exchange across the thematic categories of the PhD programme. It addressed key issues of research, establishing shared terms of reference and cultivating essential research skills. The seminar concluded with an introduction to the notion of performance in architecture, a critical concept for both research and architectural practice, that will be taken up as a key topic for the seminar next term.

Visiting Theory
Seminar, February
2006, with Tony
Vidler (right) and
Mark Cousins (left).

Continuing Research Projects

Pedro Ignacio Alonso
*The Heterogeneous Product: Four
Strategies on the Rhetoric of Assemblage*
This research is concerned with a series
of arguments which were fundamental
in the modernist conceptualisation of
architecture as a work of assemblage:
a technical-theoretical device,
an utmost idealisation of the 'new
unity' of design, construction, industry,
and economy. The relationship between
certain formulations of thought in
Sigfried Giedion's 'Bauen in Frankreich,
Eisen, Eisenbeton' (1928) and Konrad
Wachsmann's 'Wendepunkt im Bauen'
(1959) is a case study for the investigation.

M.L. Chittawadi Chitrabongs
*Cleanliness in Thailand: The 'Strategy of
Hygiene' from Urban Planning to Lavatories dating from the Mid-19th Century*
The research examines the political
history of the Thai Royal Family and one
aspect of Siam's modernisation, namely
public health and hygiene reforms.
It argues that the infrastructure of water
supply, modern crematoria, public
lavatories and western dress codes are
introduced to Bangkok citizens not only
for public good, but also for protecting
Siam's independence from European
colonial expansion and maintaining the
royal influence over the domain.

Tania Lopez Winkler
*Clues in the Detection of London: Evidence
of the Construction of Knowledge of the
City in 19th-Century London*
The project draws upon two main
sources: government statistics for 19th-
century London, and the detective novel
as a register of the city (and ways of
living), from which the clue is enacted as
a cross-sectional device that enables us
to operate at different levels.

Komson Teeraparbwong
Revisiting Critical Regionalism
The assimilation of traditional and
modern dwellings within the city of
Chiang Mai, Thailand

Claudio Araneda
*Dis-Information in the Cities of the
Information Age*

Hua Li
Sinification: Fantasies of the 'Western Modern' in Contemporary Chinese Architecture and Urbanism
The thesis provides a conceptual interpretation of how the imports from Europe and the USA are appropriated and contribute to architectural production in China since the late 1970s. It argues that 'westernisation' is a misleading account for the whole process. The architecture and urbanism which are demanded by modernity and are product of modernisation in China are not usefully regarded as 'western' or 'non-western'.

Kaarina-Nancy Bauer
Heinrich Wölfflin
In this historiographical analysis of Heinrich Wölfflin his theories, texts, and issues provide a case study that illuminates continuing problems, paradoxes, and questions in the ongoing discourse of the discipline of art history.

Jose Gregorio Brugnoli
The Transformation of the House through the Development of Electromechanical Appliances

Frances Mikuriya
Time Space Pathologies

Pablo Leon Barra Vargas
Art and Architecture:
The Creation of Space and Place in Contemporary Art

Enrique Walker
The Infra-Ordinary City:
George Perec's Lieux Project

Research Group on Architectural Urbanism

The seminar on architectural urbanism aims to define a common intellectual terrain among the participating research students, promoting their ability to debate issues emerging from their individual thesis work in relation to the broader field. Together, the students are pursuing a distinctive style of

reasoning about architecture's role within a strategic urbanism, emphasising both a historically informed approach to contemporary architectural trends and a refusal of stable and contextualist understandings of the urban.

Katharina Borsi
Urban Domestic:
The Diagram of the Berlin Block
The Berlin block emerged in the 1860s as an instrument which enabled a continuously articulated reasoning about the elements of the city linked to the project of building. Its efficacy as a diagram lay in its relatively complete consideration of the urban across scales and dimensions while also supporting the differentiation of urban life. Seen in this way the diagram persists as a deep structure of urban transformation even in 20th-century patterns of functional segregation, opening the way for new socio-spatial concepts.

Tarsha Finney
Repetition and Transformation:
The Housing project and the constitution of the urban field
Through the specificity of the housing project in mid-20th-century New York, this research will examine notions of transformation and reasoning through change. Here, the housing project is understood as process, constitutive of a field of dispute and experimentation. Architectural change is always simultaneously diagnostic and propositional, questioning both the function of dwelling and the notion of the city itself.

Pavlos Philippou
Cultivating Urbanism: The diagram of contemporary cultural institutions
Beginning in the late 19th century and becoming codified by the early 20th century, cultural buildings came to acquire a salient role in urban reasoning. Cultivating Urbanism pursues this reasoning through two distinct but interrelated themes. Firstly, their spatial and organisational structure, or typology, established a consistent

platform for architectural and urban transformation. Secondly, a governmental rationality regarding the role of culture in the formation of urban subjects traverses their diagram as urban cultural institutions.

New PhD Projects

Doreen Bernath
From the Image, the Imaged, to the Imaginative: A Section through the Production, Function and Implication of Images in Contemporary Chinese Architecture

Nerma Cridge
War and Architecture Underground: Visions, Utopias and Fantasies

Valeria Guzmán-Verri
Faragraphism: Destinations through the Great Number

Dong Ku Kim
Sustainable Kinetic Design for Korean Climate

Rosalea Monacella
Landscape Productions: The Emergent Grid for a Dynamic Contemporary Metropolis

Kristine Mun
Morphological Essences: From Abstract Materialism to Sense History

Jose Tovar Barrientos
The Region as an Operative Field

Manika Khosla
Programmatic and Urban Strategies for High-Density Housing within Global Economies in the 21st Century

Final Year & Completions

John H. Abell
Desiring Spatialities – Architectural Effects: On the Architectural Exposé of Psychosexual Empathy, Form and Space

Manuela Antoniu
On Hunger and the Phagic in Architecture

Nikolaos Patsavos
A History of the Present of Greek Architectural Education

Dulce Marques De Almeida
The Effect of Microclimate on the Design of Pedestrian Areas in Cities

Luciano Dutra
The Use of Environmental Information in Architectural Design

Derin Inan
From Cartography to Master Planning: The Ankara plan as an index of urban discourses in Turkey

Nikolaos Koronis
Total Work of Art in Modern Architecture

Rachel McCann
Wild Being and Carnal Echo: An Application of Merleau-Ponty's Theory of Intersubjectivity to the Design and Experience of Architecture

Marcelo Espinosa Martinez
The Architecture of Negative Realities

Ludwig Abache
The Contested Space of the Highway: An Inquiry into the Transformation of Public Space, the Case of La Autopista, Caracas, Venezuela

Rosa Schiano-Phan
The Development of Passive Downdraught Evaporative Cooling Systems Using Porous Ceramic Evaporators and their Application in Residential Buildings

Hooke Park visit, Introduction Week,
October 2005 (photo Paloma Diaz)

Complementary Courses

History & Theory Studies

General Studies is dead; long live History and Theory Studies. The change in title accompanied Brett Steele's assumption of the directorship of the AA. Certainly there was no virtue in 'General Studies'. It sounded like Residual Studies or possibly Religious Studies, courses that were damp with neglect. And History and Theory Studies? At least the title is accurate, but if the change is to have any value, it should lie in a reassessment of the relation between HTS and the rest of the School. We have tried to do that this year, to project a new role for HTS on the basis of an analysis of other changes within the School. The first application of this will appear in the Intermediate School, which in 2006/07, will have a syllabus and objectives which are quite different from preceding years.

Firstly the analysis. There are features of the School which make it difficult for HTS to operate. Students pass through the Intermediate School with a strong sense that the central core of their work and their architectural progress lie in their unit work. At the same time those units propose programmes which are much more theoretical than in the past. This 'theory' is a heterogeneous series of discourses – sometimes the theories are drawn from the natural sciences, from morphogenic studies, from arguments within geometry, from social theories. This 'heterogeneity' should not mask the fact, however, that they play a relatively defined role and function within the unit and even articulate the differences between units.

We might start here in defining a productive role for HTS. At the moment students hear of many terms whose meaning and provenance are unknown to them. Marina Lathouri and I taught a transitional course in Theory in 2005/06 to the Third Year students. We were not investigating esoteric concepts, but what we might call architectural categories. They included Form, Tectonics, Function, Scale and Size, and Geometry. The students felt they did not know the 'real' meaning of the terms,

and because of that felt excluded from a number of discussions in the School. They seemed relieved that the purpose of the course was not to provide 'meanings' to the categories, but to recognise that each category included a number of conflicting, contested terms, and that to understand architectural discussion it was important to recognise the different sense in which each category can be discussed. To put this more formally, the task of theory within HTS is to expand the students' comprehension of conventional architectural categories and put them into a relation with their unit's use of concepts.

Over the years there has been a great deal of discussion about architectural history and its role in the curriculum. We have to acknowledge that many of our students don't see the point in studying it. Much of the problem lies with the discipline of architectural history; its issues reflect those of art history, rather than architecture. Nor is it clear that the complex issue of the relation of the architect to architecture's past is best studied as a historical problem. History is a form of knowledge which conventionally links narrative and causality and thereby privileges the question of influence. 'Narrative' and 'influence' are not the first categories which would seem relevant to an architecture student. Broadly speaking, the question is whether we think architectural history is an important dimension for the contemporary architectural student. My point is that even if it is, this must be argued, and the forms of its presentation must be considered. To take an obvious case: when students study or review architecture of the past, they are concerned with far more issues than 'historical' problems. They look at past architecture as a precedent and use it to express their own architectural identity, just as a lawyer labours over the field of common law as a precedent – not to repeat the past but to find in the precedent the reason to do something different.

This brings us to the most radical reorganisation – that of the First Year. We have decided, and have experimented this year with the idea that HTS should start at the beginning; that is with architectural representation. The issues of the plan, the section, the elevation, the sketch and various practices of drawing, not to mention the question of the computer and digital design, all have a history, all have certain effects, and all can be challenged theoretically. Our intention is to introduce them at the beginning of the First Year, so that students do not experience them as neutral, eternal technical devices, but as objects which have a historical and critical dimension.

The second half of the First Year will be devoted to another problem which goes to the heart of our students' difficulty with their architectural education. How do you describe architecture in words? Students will be taken to certain buildings and asked to give an analysis of the building in words. This itself permits a building up of case studies, which assists the future course on architecture and its past.

The course, in this year of transition, has been strengthened by the inclusion amongst its teachers of a number of PhD students. Frances Mikuriya, Pedro Ignacio Alonso, Christiane Fashek and Theo Spyropoulos have been invaluable in replanning the course. Equally helpful have been Marina Lathouri and Tim Brittain-Catlin. Irénée Scalbert, who has taught in Intermediate for many years, will now move to the Diploma School in order to teach a course in Architectural Criticism, a topic which he has long wanted to foster at the AA. This review hardly mentions the Diploma School since it is the Intermediate School which is changing. There will be time enough next year to describe the changes we make there. But we should not end without thanking its teachers and without expressing our enduring gratitude to Belinda Flaherty, without whom none of these courses would work.

Mark Cousins

In addition to a very active year of evening lectures, symposia, conferences and open seminars, the History & Theory studies programme offered the following courses: Architectural Knowledge, Building the Modern City, Modern Architectural Concepts, Mechanical Dreams & Digital Fantasies, The Architectural Dream Work – 1900–2000, Junk, Pattern City, The AA Before Yesterday, Formalism Now, Peter Pan and Wendy Houses, Reflections on Water, Meaning & Modes of Architectural Representation, Towards the Archipelago, Beyond the Stasis, Energy, Environment, Architecture & the City, The Pain of Time Past, Pre-Digital/Post-Digital.

Staff: Mark Cousins (Director), Pedro Ignacio Alonso, Pier Vittorio Aureli, Timothy Brittain-Catlin, Mark Campbell, Paul Davies, William Firebrace, Brian Hatton, Andrew Higgott, Marina Lathouri, George L Legendre, Frances H Mikuriya, Sandra Morris, Irénée Scalbert, Pascal Schöning, Brett Steele, Dalibor Vesely, Simos Yannas

Media Studies

The Media Studies programme provides a wide range of courses that address the multi-faceted complexity of architectural project execution. As methods of production, analysis and communication are constantly being reassessed, Media Studies attempts to include a spectrum of techniques that both reinforce and reinvent the methods by which students approach design and architecture. This year's courses include media from video, photography and drawing to physical assemblages and computer-based projects.

Department Head: Eugene Han

Department Staff: Sue Barr (Black+White Photography, Colour Digital Photography), Valentin Bontjes Van Beek (Drawing Seeing Drawing, Object Fabrication), Monia De Marchi (Precision Modelling Workshop), Shin Egashira (One-To-One Instruments, Translation Object to Drawing), Christian Grou (Digital Film, 3D Animation), Eugene Han (Digital Visualisation/Integration, Customised Computation), Katrin Lahusen (Going Baroque 2, 3D Games), Antoni Malinowski (Large Scale Drawing, Materiality of Colour), Joel Newman (Video, Digital Video), Anne Save de Beaurecueil (Curve Networks, Beyond the Wireframe), Goswin Schwendinger (Colour Photography), Tapio Snellman (Digital Film, 3D Animation), Vasilis Stroumpakos (Code Engines, Screen Interface), David Tortora (Interactive Media)

Patrick Usborne: Customised Computation

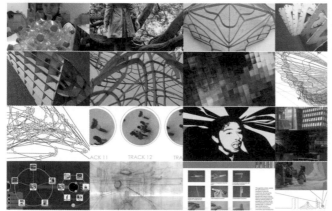

Opposite page
Top: Selected student works throughout the year
Bottom: First Year Final Jury, Autumn

Naiara Vegara
Colour Photography, Autumn

Technical Studies

The Technical Studies programme begins with the acknowledgement that it must be sensitive to the local demands of the unit agendas, while it must also construct a complete and coherent technical education that extends over five years, building up a substantial knowledge base that engages with the practices and intellectual dialogues of material productions in the world. The programme continues to evolve from detailed discussions with lecturers, all of whom are drawn from leading engineering practices and research institutions, and who between them are engaged in a wide range of disciplines and current projects. Knowledge developed from critical case studies of current material processes, constructed artefacts and buildings includes critical reflection and experimentation with the ideas and techniques.

Lecture courses form a portion of each year's requirements. In the Second and Fourth Years students concentrate on critical case studies, analysis and material experiments in two courses. In First Year and Third Year, lecture coursework, workshop experiments and technical ambitions are developed. Students undertake design research and experiments to explore and resolve the technical issues of their main projects. In the Fifth Year, students undertake a Technical Design Thesis, a substantial individual work developed under the guidance of Technical Studies. The Thesis is contextualised as part of a broader dialogue in which technical and architectural agendas are synthesised, and its critical development is pursued through case studies, material experiments and extensive research and consultation.

Staff: Michael Weinstock (Master of Technical Studies), Wolf Mangelsdorf, Simon Beames, Nikolaos Stathopoulos (Diploma Tutors), Javier Castanon (Intermediate Master), Wolfgang Frese, Nikolaos Stathopoulos (Intermediate Tutors)

First Year Structures Competition
The First Year Structures course taught by Philip Cooper and Anderson Inge culminates in the annual Spaghetti Structure Competition, for which students collaborate in the design, fabrication and load-testing of their triangulated structures. Here students apply the theory and analytic methods taught in the series of lectures that forms the backbone of the course. The brief for the competition has required a 'lean-to' structure capable of sustaining a considerable rolling load, which induces quite different stresses as it moves through different positions on the structure.

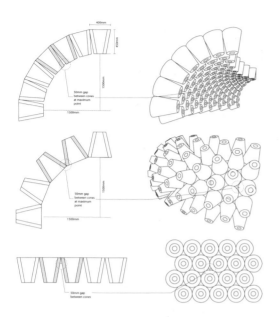

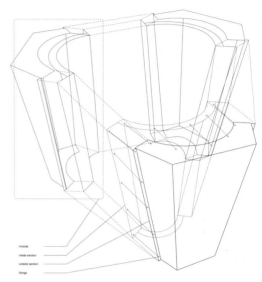

Martin Jameson, Intermediate Unit 3
ICA Rooftop Gallery
The gallery uses a simple module —
a truncated cone, or frustum — to create
a range of lighting effects. The cone is packed
into a hexagonal configuration and then
manipulated into a continuous surface.
The amount of natural light in each space is
controlled by the cone aperture and length;
light quality is controlled by the cone
orientation.

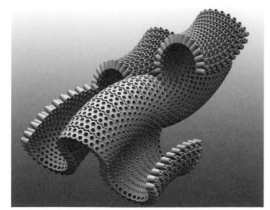

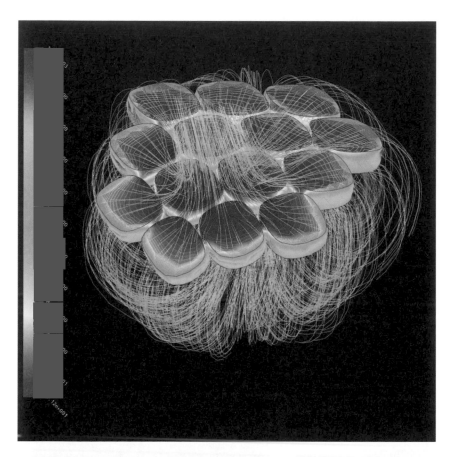

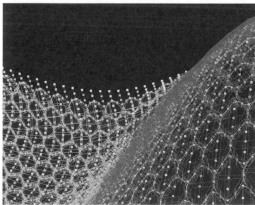

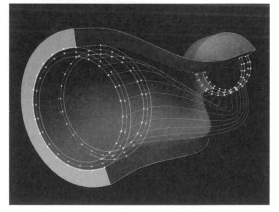

Defne Sunguroglu, Diploma Unit 4
Complex Brick Assemblies
The project seeks to further develop the geometric repertoire achieved through techniques used by Eladio Dieste, working towards complex double-curved prestressed brick assemblies that do not rely on additional mortar and the concrete shell for stability, which enables the structural surface to be porous. Control curves, rod members and bricks inform the structural, environmental and spatial performance capacites. Differentiation of the bricks, assembly processes and their spatial arrangement results in complex, heterogeneous and differentiated micro and macro environments for habitation.

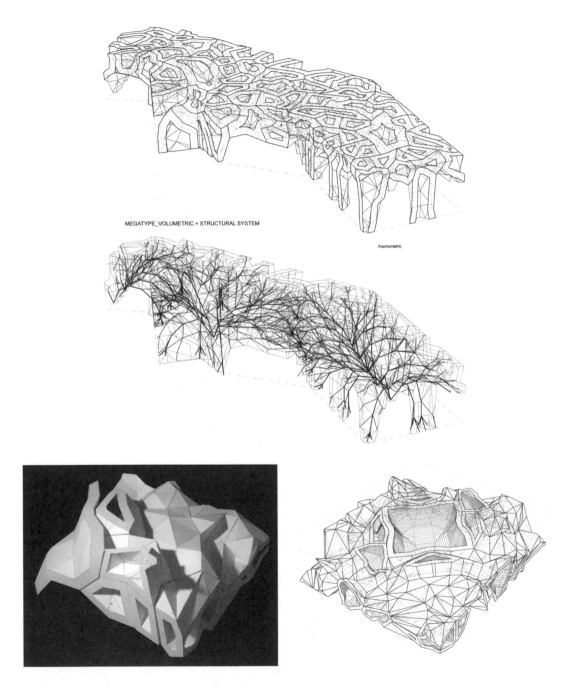

MEGATYPE_VOLUMETRIC + STRUCTURAL SYSTEM

Axonometric

Valeria Segovia, Diploma Unit 6
Structural Arteries
The project explores two ways of developing a collective type that compresses programme within a mass.
Both prototypes (Branching Model and Voronoi Model) are developed by articulating the voids. The Megatype is
regulated by the voids and the way they are circulated and serviced. The arterial structural system compresses
circulation and services of the overall building. The passages are the primary structural arteries that stabilise the
whole structure and conduct the flow in and out of the site.

AA Workshops

The AA Workshops, which include the
Workshop, Model Shop and Hooke Park,
give students the opportunity to work
with a broad variety of materials and
techniques on the way to discovering
methods of combining design and
applications. Students are encouraged
to explore materials and their use as
much as develop lateral thinking and
problem-solving skills. Facilities in the
Bedford Square premises include
machine and hand tools for working
in steel and some nonferrous metals,
and for precise working in hardwoods,
softwoods and panel products, as well
as for working in stone, concrete,
ferrocement and some plastics and
composites. A link with the Computing
Lab and the introduction of a Multitool
Changing CNC-routing machine
enables work to be produced directly
from computer drawings and virtual
designs, joining up-to-date production
techniques with traditional craft skills.
Work produced varies in scale and type
from small site models, in the Model
Shop, to large conceptual pieces, in both
the Bedford Square and Hooke Park
workshops.

Workshop Manager: Marcellus Letang,
Assistant Manager: Trystrem Smith,
Technician: Jon Cole, Model Workshop:
David King, Workshop Tutor: Andreas
Lang, Hooke Park Workshop: Charlie
Corry Wright

Student Assistants: Jesse Sabatier,
Jesse Randzio, Julia King, Sergey
Kudryashev

Clockwise from top left: Two views of Workshop (photo Valerie Bennett); Model Shop (photo Chris Fenn); Model Shop (photo Valerie Bennett); Ching's Yard (photo Valerie Bennett).

Hooke Park, the AA's outpost in Dorset, is a 350-acre woodland site whose facilities have long included an institute for researching new uses for working in wood. Under the AA's management, this has been extended to encompass all kinds of future material concepts, as well as the promotion of experimental sustainable construction. The spacious facilities and outdoor environment provide a setting for workshops and projects that might be problematic to carry out in the confines of Central London. Students are able to explore techniques ranging from model-making to object fabrication and prototyping, and to produce work on a much larger scale, supported by specialist staff based at the site. Here Intermediate Unit 2 construct the AA Summer Pavilion prior to installation in Bedford Square, a project supported by Finnforest UK, Maeda Corporation, Arup AGU, Architen Landrell and *Building Design*.

AA Visiting Programmes

Participation in the academic life of the AA is not limited to full-time enrolment. Several shorter Visiting Programmes attract those who come not just to participate in, but also contribute to, the School's lively architectural culture. Each programme has been tailored to a different length of study, topic and focus, offering a full range of academic and professional possibilities for experiencing the AA School. See aaschool.ac.uk for further information.

The curriculum for this year's Spring Visiting Students programme focused on translating methods of producing fiction into architectural strategies. We investigated the relationship between architecture and film based on the methodology of the comic. All three practices provide temporal experiences, often fractured, always highly dependent on the creation of meaning through the use of space and established modes of perception. We considered the architectural within the drawing of the comic and its subsequent translation into blockbusters, discussing the shared structural elements as well as the discrete specificities and restraints that these fields maintain.

In the studio we attempted to develop alternative spatial diagrams from these fictional constructs and their subsequent application and adaptation into real space by exploring the potential of comics and films to contaminate traditional static ideas of architectural space.

We analysed three movies (*Hulk*, *Batman Begins*, *Sin City*) and transferred their operative methodologies and organisational logics into relational diagrams and 3d tactics that generated potential new spatial realities, culminating in proposals for a pavilion for the London Comic and Film Festival.

Programme Staff: Oliver Domeisen, Sam Jacoby, Monia De Marchi

Students: Andrew Ashey, Jean Choi, Ellen Gedopt, Xiaoxian Huay, Seokwon Kim, Annette Sanne, Sydney Schwartz

Above: Andrew Ashey, Sin Pavilion – Sin City
Right: Xiaoxian Huay, Spatial Edits – The Hulk

AA Workshop, June 2006
(photo Valerie Bennett)

Associations

Research Clusters

In 2005/06 the AA launched four new research clusters as a way of connecting the work of different units, programmes and courses not only to one another but also to a larger world of outside expertise, interest and support. The clusters seek to create the circumstances of a more open, intelligent and adaptive organisation of the AA, initiating a generational evolution of the School's now-stable unit structure. This change aims to reinterpret the AA's own organisation and operation, like its pedagogies, course contents and student output, as unique within the world of contemporary architecture schools. The clusters will evolve over the coming years according to the declared interests of the members of our School Community.

Each of these new clusters is curated by members of the School Community and given support from the Director's Office. The curators' role is to offer necessary communication points for coordinating events that take place as part of each cluster, including visiting lectures, open seminars, short-term workshops, publications, site visits and other activities that go beyond the scope of individual units or courses.

Alternative Practices Research Initiatives (APRI) Cluster

The remit of this research cluster is operative and strategic, touching upon modes of studying, teaching and working in architecture. We believe there are many models of what might follow on from a five-year architectural education at the AA, and different alternatives to entering an established architectural office. These might include setting up practices in the form of multidisciplinary collectives, becoming part of international networks, or embarking on practice-based or academic research, to name just a few.

At the same time we believe that there are possibilities of looking at alternative models linking education to practice over the course of the five-year period. This cluster provides an opportunity to expose such synergies of architectural education and practice.

We brought together speakers from within the AA and beyond to discuss key topics, defined through discussions at the start of the year.

To address different models of arts and architectural residencies, we had Erland Blakstad Haffner (Fantastic Norway), Clare Cumberlidge (General Public Agency), Theo Lorenz (Dip 14), Frances Morrell (Arts Inform), Barbara Stevini (O+I), and Rob Wilson (RIBA).

For the 'Live Projects' panel we invited Prue Chiles (Sheffield University), Shin Egashira (Dip 11), Hugo Hinsley (AA Graduate School), Robert Mull (London Metropolitan University), and Hana Loftus (speaking about Rural Studio). They all presented current and past experiences of live projects in a range of contexts, initiating a useful discussion about the issues, problems and benefits for schools, students, clients and the community.

The final event of the year focused on 'Academic Research', discussing the AA's current capacity and experience, and the possibilities for further development. Speakers on this panel were Allan Cochrane (Open University), Michael Keith (Goldsmiths), Andy Pratt (LSE), and Simos Yannas and Larry Barth (AA Graduate School).

A fourth theme will be addressed next year, through an event focusing on 'Year Out' experiences, raising awareness of different alternatives, sharing past experiences and discussing what type of support might be needed.

Additional activities included a session with First Year students and tutors, and participation in a 'Designing for the Twenty-first Century' symposium organised by two of the main UK research councils.

Cluster Curators: Susana Gonzalez, Andreas Lang

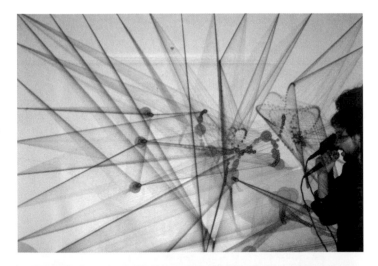

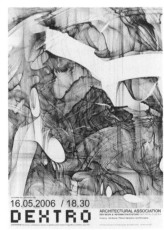

16.05.2006 / 18.30
DEXTRO   ARCHITECTURAL ASSOCIATION

LAPTOP
JAM
SESSIONS
18.05.2006 / 18.30   ARCHITECTURAL ASSOCIATION

Clockwise from top left: Laptop jam
sessions, posters for Dextro and
Laptop jam sessions, students
participating in Stelarc performance
(all New Media cluster events), APRI
cluster 'Live Projects' panel.

Architectural Urbanism, Social and Political Space (AUSP) Cluster

In its first year, the research cluster Architectural Urbanism, Social and Political Space is still in the process of defining its operations. Conceived as a mechanism of communication, a test bed for collaborations and fertilisations across units and programmes, and possibly as a way of establishing research links with the outside, the cluster continues to experiment with the definition and scope of its activities. The themes indicated in the cluster title are relevant to many units and programmes within the AA. As curators, we believe that this cluster in particular should be driven from within the existing activities and interests of the School.

Events / Term 2
Scales and/of Engagement I/II
Two open discussion sessions explored a salient point of discussion triggered by the AA Open Jury: what are the relationships between Scale and Engagement in dealing with the contemporary city?

From interventions on a regional scale to 1:1 proposals that activate a local space, the range of interventions undertaken at the AA render the urban as a terrain marked by continued contestation. Our engagement with the urban – through the tools, techniques and means of representation – is defined by the terrain of our analysis as well as the scale of intervention. This research cluster proposes to open and scrutinise the discussion across these scales. By juxtaposing positions and approaches that exist in the School, the aim was not so much to emphasise distinct, territorial positions, but to collectively compare the many ways in which the AA currently addresses the problem of the city.

The sessions involved short presentations from tutors and students from Dip 2, Dip 6, Dip 10, Dip 15, Inter 10, Landscape and Urbanism and Histories and Theories, followed by a convivial discussion/debate, chaired by the cluster curators and guests. These sessions were open to the entire School.

Through individual presentations around the theme of scale and engagement, a productive discussion about the very definition of terms and approaches developed. The debate about increased communication between units and programmes concerning questions of the urban, should be taken in itself as a productive outcome. In terms of language, we might have opened up as many differences as commonalities across the School. Those approaches that take scale as a concept defined by the body and governed by a set of interests deal with an entirely different set of questions to those pedagogies that assume scale to be a given category within urbanism. On the other hand, in the graphic work, there is some potential for interesting overlaps.

Publication
To allow these discussions to be disseminated, we felt it important to crystallise them into a publication that would also provide a snap–shot of this period in the School's understanding of these topics. This publication could also be referred to by future curators as the starting point of the cluster's activity. Designed by Kasia Korczak and edited by a group of MA Histories and Theories students, the publication was produced with the speed of a magazine and the feel of an intimate bulletin for the School Community.

Term 3
Scales and/of Engagement, Part III:
Leit-Werk and Information Based
Architecture
A presentation focused on two
significant XL projects by AA alumni.
Mark Hemel, of Information Based
Architecture, talked about his
experiences in winning and facilitating
what will be one of the world's tallest
buildings: the 610-metre-high TV &
Sightseeing Tower in Guangzhou, China.
Leit-Werk's Henrik Rothe discussed the
complex relationships between
architect, client and experts in the
masterplanning of their proposal for a
new airport in Sudan's capital city,
Kharthoum. Discussion ensued upon
the role of the architect's engagement
in projects of such scale, as well as the
political dimension of architecture
operating in these cultural geographies.

Forthcoming in Autumn 2006:
Cities from Zero
'Cities from Zero' is conceived as a
symposium that deals with new twenty-
first-century forms of urbanism that
occur where there is no ostensible
precedent or urban history from which
to start. China, Dubai, and possibly
Africa, will figure as sites for the
symposium's scrutiny – sites that have
been and will continue to be of
importance to the AA.

Cluster Curators: Shumon Basar,
Katharina Borsi

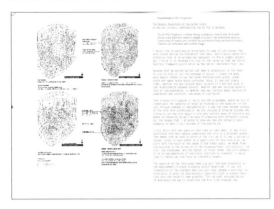

Right, top three images: Spreads from the
AUSP cluster's publication, 'A Document of
Scales and/of Engagement'.
Bottom: Cynthia Davidson offers an
introduction to Log in a Visiting Theory
Seminar hosted by the AUSP
(photo Valerie Bennett).

Environments, Ecologies & Sustainability (EES) Cluster

The Environments, Ecologies & Sustainability research cluster gathers, investigates and disseminates potential research questions that elicit new EES responses within design, research and pedagogy at the AA and beyond. The cluster is committed to assisting the definition of new research questions within EES design while creating forums for the collective research and debate of highlighted issues. The cluster also aims to support project-based research initiatives within the School and the AA Community. The intention is to branch out, reaching a wider association, and to open the doors to a new kind of non-architectural participant at the AA.

The EES cluster hosted the first Environmental Associations discussion in the spring of this year. This informal roundtable discussion with experts from different fields provided various viewpoints on how design can address current and future challenges caused by changing climates and increased resource consumption. The topic also covered the notion of sustainability within continually changing environmental, climatic and social conditions.

Environmental Tectonics Competition
The AA and the EES cluster are also sponsoring an open, one-stage international competition in search of innovative architectural methodologies and design-related research, working towards an understanding of environ-ments, ecology and sustainability. The competition is an open call for projects and ideas. The aim of the competition is to locate new projects that consider the larger contextual issues of environ-mental change while formulating critical and informed responses. The winner will be announced in October 2006 at the opening of the competition exhibition. For an information pack go to: www.aaschool.ac.uk/clusters/ees.shtm

Cluster Curators: Werner Gaiser, Steve Hardy

New Media and Information Systems Research Cluster

The New Media initiative views design as an open act of experimentation exploring space as interface and environment. Our pursuit of architecture seeks both digital and analogue systems of exchange; it is based on an active integration of both material and communication technologies. We conceive of space as an environment that necessitates adaptive and responsive relations to the user. The overall aim is to generate an active engagement of body–space relations.

To this end the New Media initiative has to be understood as the exploration of new technologies and their potential impact on the practice of architecture. The AA is attempting to rewrite estab-lished trains of thought, critical theories and modes of production. We wish to hasten and strengthen this process by developing links with artists, designers and thinkers from outside architecture who can reflect objectively on changes in architectural practice.

One of the aims of the cluster is to engage with the emerging domains of code-generated art, programming and simulating of behaviours, information visualisation, dynamic diagramming and interface design, which all have output into the visual. These fields create a new language and polemic that a) gives birth to a new *abstraction* that is driven by and visualises complex structured relationships rather than an *abstraction* for the sake of the shape, b) seeks *intuition* in terms of understanding, learning and communicating rather than being *intuitively* composed, c) prefers to design dynamic relationships of behaviours rather than design layouts, d) speaks of an *interface* devoid from the metaphors of the analogue age and e) comes to redefine the nature and concept of the *screen* from scratch.

Cluster Curators: Joel Newman, Theodore Spyropoulos, Vasili Stroumpakos

Top right: Stelarc performance hosted by New
Media cluster (photo Valerie Bennett).
All other photos: Environmental Associations –
Roundtable Discussion. Participants included
Steve Hardy, Werner Gaiser (EES Cluster
Curators), Klaus Bode (BDSP Partnership),
Sebastian Appl & Ulrich Beckefeld (via live link,
Office of Subversive Architecture), David Lloyd
Jones (Studio E Architects), Jane Durney
(BioRegional Consulting and One Planet
Products), Justin Wimbush (Arup), Doris
Oesterreicher (Atelier Ten), Philip Beesley
(via live link, University of Waterloo/Philip
Beesley Architects), David Dowell (via live link,
El Dorado Architects).

Clockwise from top left across spread: Autumn Term 2005 events poster, held by Tania Lopez Winkler; Graduate School 2006/07 poster, Rama Nshiewat and Tala Fustok; Summer School 2006 poster, Linjie Wang; Surface Intelligence symposium poster, Rama Nshiewat;

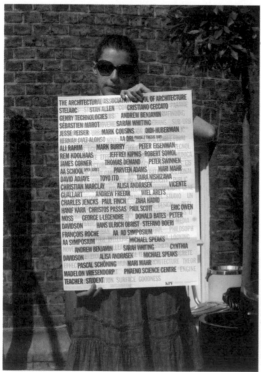

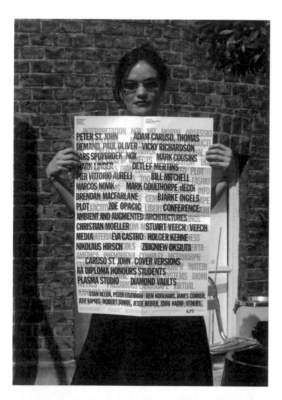

Visiting Student Programmes 2006/07 poster, Tala Fustok; DLAB 2006 poster, Sanem Alper; 'Caruso St John: Cover Versions' exhibition handout, Nikolay Shahpazov; Spring Term 2006 events poster, Valeria Guzman (posters Zak Kyes; photos Valerie Bennett).

Clockwise from top left across spread: *Manifesto for a Cinematic Architecture*, Pascal Schöning, January 2006; *AA Files 54*, July 2006; *Structure as Space*, Jürg Conzett, Mohsen Mostafavi, Bruno Reichlin, May 2006; *Diamond Vaults*, ZoĎ Opacic, November 2005;

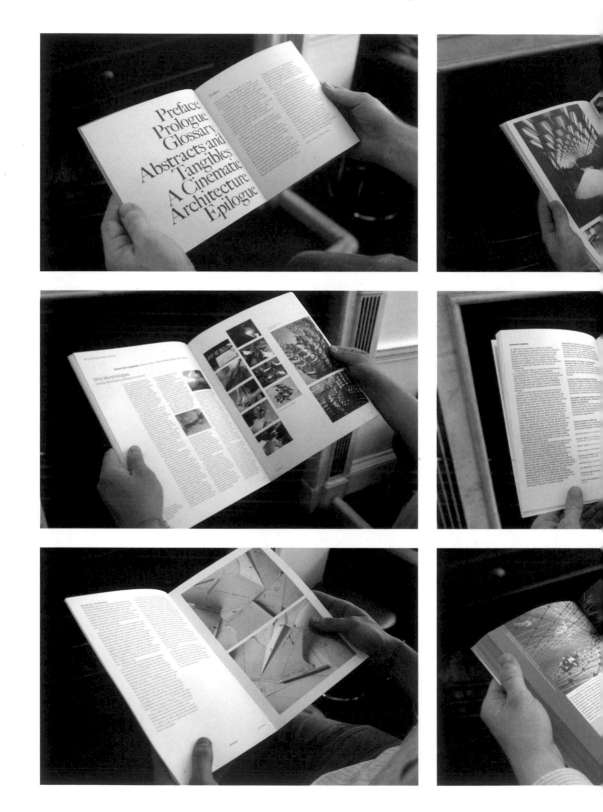

AA Publications Catalogue 2005/06; AA Projects Review, July 2005; *Bodyline*, George L Legendre, March 2006; *AA Files 53*, May 2006; AA Prospectus, October 2005 (photos Valerie Bennett).

From top: 'Cinematic Architecture' exhibition in the AA Gallery, March 2006 (photo Sue Barr) and cover of *A Manifesto for Cinematic Architecture*.

From top: 'Teacher/Student: Not the Last Word' exhibition in the Front Members' Room, February 2006 (photo Sue Barr) and alternate covers for *Bodyline*.

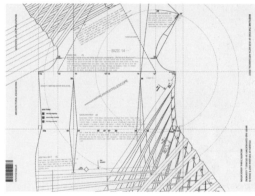

BODYLINE
THE END OF OUR
META–MECHANICAL
BODY STUDIES OF
DIPLOMA UNIT 5
2002–5 BRIEF AND
COMMENTARY BY
GEORGE L. LEGENDRE

From top: Smartslab, from the Surface Intelligence: Ambient &
Augmented Architectures symposium, November 2005 (photo Valerie
Bennett); 'Thames Gateway Assembly at the AA' exhibition, AA Gallery,
April 2006 (photo Sue Barr).

From top: AA Summer Pavilion,designed and built by Inter 2 at Hooke Park with the support of Finnforest UK, the Maeda Corporation and others, and assembled in Bedford Square June 2006 (photo Rosa Ainley); 'Plasma Studio' exhibition, AA Gallery, November 2005 (photo Chris Fenn).

'Caruso St John: Cover Versions' exhibition, AA Gallery, October 2005
(photo Chris Fenn)

'Phaeno Science Centre' exhibition, AA Gallery, February 2006
(photo Sue Barr)

AA Digital Platforms / AA Web

Digital Platforms, new to the AA this year, was created to focus on digital media. The AA DP's remit is to design and develop a series of applications that will communicate and archive schoolwork and activities, both for public use and as an internal information resource. Design and research undertaken by AA students and staff are the greatest assets of a school renowned for its cutting-edge educational approach, quality of work and experimentation. The first projects undertaken this year are the AA DVD (launched with Projects Review 2005/06) and AA Web (coming soon).

AA DVD
aaschool.ac.uk/aadvd
This year we release the first AA DVD, a digital component of the AA Projects Review publication. With more than 4,000 images and 80 videos, it presents approximately 360 projects from Foundation and First Year, and the Intermediate, Diploma and Graduate schools, as well as material from this year's Lectures, Exhibitions and Publications. The AA DVD is the first step in a long-term project: the creation of the AA Archive, a digital archive of the School's best work.

AA LOG
aalog.net
In September 2005 the school launched AA LOG, an informal, continuously updated diary of school life to which AA staff contribute news, images and notes.

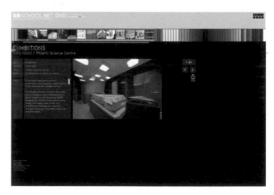

AA Website
aaschool.ac.uk
The current AA website was designed five years ago. We are currently redesigning it, with the aim of making the School's work its most prominent component.

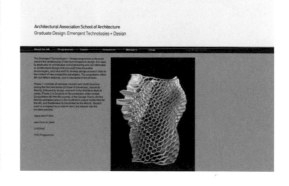

AA Intermediate and Diploma School end-of-year review tables,
June 2006 (photos Valerie Bennett)

Director
Brett Steele

Foundation
Miraj Ahmed
Theo Lorenz
Saskia Lewis

First Year
Valentin Bontjes
 van Beek
David Greene
Alex Haw
Nicholas Puckett
Nathalie Rozencwajg
Martina Schäfer

**Intermediate
School**

Unit 1
Peter Salter
Stefano Rabolli
 Pansera

Unit 2
Charles Walker
Martin Self

Unit 3
Natasha Sandmeier
Monia De Marchi

Unit 4
Mark Hemel
Nate Kolbe

Unit 6
Veronika Schmid
Alistair Gill

Unit 7
Markus Miessen
Matthew Murphy

Unit 8
Yusuke Obuchi
Eugene Han

Unit 9
Shumon Basar
Oliver Domeisen

Unit 10
Kathrin Böhm
Andreas Lang

Diploma School

Unit 1
Charles Tashima
Tyen Masten

Unit 2
Anne Save de
 Beaurecueil
Franklin Lee

Unit 3
Pascal Schöning
Rubens Azevedo
Julian Löffler

Unit 4
Michael Hensel
Achim Menges

Unit 6
Chris Lee
Sam Jacoby

Unit 8
Chiafang Wu
Stephen Roe

Unit 9
John Bell
Adam Covell

Unit 10
Carlos Villanueva
 Brandt

Unit 11
Shin Egashira

Unit 12
Eva Castro
Holger Kehne

Unit 13
Philippe Rahm
Alex Haw

Unit 14
Theo Lorenz
Neil Davidson
Peter Staub

Unit 15
Francesca Hughes
Rita Lambert

Unit 16
Steve Hardy
Jonas Lundberg

Graduate School

Graduate Design:
AADRL
Yusuke Obuchi
Patrik Schumacher
Theodore
 Spyropoulos
Tom Verebes
Programme Staff
Tom Barker
Christiane Fashek
Hanif Kara
George L Legendre
Djordje Stojanovic
Vasilis Stroumpakos

Graduate Design:
Emtech
Michael Weinstock
Michael Hensel
Achim Menges
Martin Hemberg

Histories & Theories
Mark Cousins
Katharina Borsi
Marina Lathouri
Robert Maxwell

Housing & Urbanism
Jorge Fiori
Lawrence Barth
Nicholas Bullock
Hugo Hinsley
Dominic Papa
Elena Pascolo
Carlos Villanueva
 Brandt

Graduate Design:
Landscape Urbanism
Eva Castro
Lawrence Barth
Sandra Morris
Leyre Asensio Villoria
David Mah
Eduardo Rico

Sustainable
Environmental Design
Simos Yannas
Klaus Bode
Werner Gaiser
Raul Moura
Peter Sharratt

Building
Conservation
John Redmill
Alan Greening
Andrew Shepherd
Sue Blundell

Landscape
Conservation &
Change
David Jacques
Axel Griesinger
Jan Woudstra

PhD Programme
Simos Yannas
Lawrence Barth
Andrew Benjamin
Nicholas Bullock
Mark Cousins
Jorge Fiori
Hugo Hinsley
Marina Lathouri
Peter Sharratt
Brett Steele

**Complementary
Courses**

History & Theory
Studies
Mark Cousins
Timothy Brittain-
 Catlin
Brian Hatton
Andrew Higgott
Marina Lathouri
Sandra Morris
Irénée Scalbert
Pascal Schöning
Dalibor Vesely
Consultants
Pedro Ignaclo Alonso
Pier Vittorio Aureli
Mark Campbell
Paul Davies
William Firebrace
George L Legendre
Frances H Mikuriya
Brett Steele
Simos Yannas

Media Studies
Eugene Han
Sue Barr
Valentin Bontjes
 van Beek
Shin Egashira
Christian Grou
Katrin Lahusen
Antoni Malinowski
Joel Newman
Anne Save de
 Beaurecueil
Goswin
Schwendinger
Tapio Snellman
Vasilis Stroumpakos
David Tortora

Professional Practice
Alastair Robertson
Part 1
Javier CastaÉon
Future Practice
Hugo Hinsley

Technical Studies
Michael Weinstock
Simon Beames
Javier CastaÉon
Phil Cooper
Wolfgang Frese
Anderson Inge
Wolf Mangelsdorf
Nikolaos
 Stathopoulos
Consultants
Carolina Bartram
Ian Duncombe
Randall Thomas
Simos Yannas
Mohsen Zikri

Workshop
Marcellus Letang
Trystrem Smith
Jon Cole

Model Shop
David King

Hooke Park
Bruce Hunter-Inglis
Charles Corry Wright
Chris Sadd

Development & Sponsorship

Since its foundation in 1847, the AA has remained both independent and self-supporting. A pioneering higher-educational charitable environment, it receives no statutory funding for the running of the School or its associated programme of public events, lectures and exhibitions.

Support, both financial and in-kind, is vital in helping the AA to provide the best architectural education and opportunities for our students. Within the Development Department the emphasis is to cultivate mutually beneficial relationships with individuals, organisations, institutions and corporate companies. A great strength of the AA is the sense of loyalty and involvement felt by the supporters who help to realise its full range of activities.

2005/06 has been a successful year for units achieving support for their work. Diploma Unit 14 worked in partnership and gained funding from Buro Happold and Buckley Gray Yeoman for their acclaimed Thames Gateway Project and subsequent exhibition. Diploma Unit 9 was assisted by the London Development Agency in realising their Crystal Palace Project. Bentley Software Systems have continued their support of the work being carried out within Emergent Technologies & Design. Adams Kara Taylor and Gehry Technologies have assisted in the ground-breaking research work achieved within the AA's Design Research Lab.

Other AA projects in 2005/06 have worked in successful partnership with industry in the UK and abroad. Intermediate Unit 2's AA Summer Pavilion Project, which made great use of the AA's Hooke Park facilities, has been supported by Arup, Finnforest, Maeda Corporation, Architen Landrell, Gardiner & Theobald and media sponsor, *Building Design* magazine. AA students also volunteered to create a design project and event for the London Architectural Biennale 2006. Their public 'Social Cinema' project was an installation and cinematic experience that took place within the outdoor venue of the Scoop Amphitheatre, adjacent to City Hall. The project attracted a broad group of sponsors and supporters including the RIBA London, More London, Camden Architects Forum, Verseidag, the British Film Institute, SGB and Fluid Structures.

During 2005/06 AA exhibitions received generous sponsorship from Blueprint magazine, Brompton Bicycles Ltd, the Concrete Centre, Corus, the Czech Centre, Dar Al Handasah UK, InBev, Icon magazine, MOORAC, PLUK, Silken Hotel Group, Sonagol, and Venturer.

We are also extremely grateful to KPF for their continued funding support for the AA's acclaimed public evening lecture programme. Generous funding support has been provided by HOK

International and Davis Langdon for our end of year Projects Review exhibition.

Hooke Park was given substantial funding in 2005/06 by the legacy executors of Mr AV Custerson. The AA was also able to establish the AV Custerson Award for Hooke Park. This has enabled AA tutors Valentin Bontjes van Beek and Nathalie Rozencwajg to initiate an ambitious Summer School, 'Bridging Hooke Park'. The project has also attracted additional funding from Dorset 'Chalk & Cheese' and the DEfRA AONB fund. The AA at Hooke Park is being viewed as vital to the regeneration of the area and has been included in strategic business plans for Dorset District and County Councils.

The AA's Scholarship & Bursary Programme also received a boost as Adams Kara Taylor pledged to continue their one-term scholarship. SOM recently pledged to begin a one-term scholarship including a paid internship starting in 2006/07. Bursary initiatives next year will include raising funding for the AA's Cedric Price Bursary.

Developing outside sponsorship and support is crucial for ensuring that the AA retains its reputation at the forefront of schools of architecture, attracting the very best students in the world.

If you are interested in discussing becoming a support partner of the AA in 2006/07 please contact:
Nicky Wynne, Development Director
Tel. 020 7887 4090
nickyw@aaschool.ac.uk

The AA would like to use this opportunity to give special thanks to the following sponsors for the substantial support they have provided in 2005/06:

KPF
www.kpf.com

HOK International Limited
www.hok.com

Davis Langdon
www.davislangdon.com

Arup
www.arup.com

Finnforest
www.finnforest.co.uk

Adams Kara Taylor
www.akt-uk.com

Buro Happold
www.burohappold.com

Gardiner & Theobald
www.gardiner.com

Architen Landrell Associates Ltd
www.architen.com

Maeda Corporation
www.maeda.co.jp

Adams Kara Taylor

Buro Happold

 Gardiner & Theobald

ARCHITEN LANDRELL ASSOCIATES

MAEDA

21 February 2006
Vicente Guallart
Media, Mountains & Architecture
Evening lecture

21 February 2006
Alisa Andrasek
Probablistic Programming
Visiting design technique seminars

22 February 2006
Andrew Freear
Rural Studio: Design through Making in Small-Town America
Evening lecture

23 February 2006
Wiel Arets
Concrete Plasticity: A Review of the University Library Utrecht 1997/2004
Lunchtime lecture

23 February 2006
Charles Jencks
Paul Finch
The Iconic Building: A Transitory or Permanent Condition?
Evening lecture

27 February 2006
Bill Odell/HOK
Sustainable Design
Evening lecture

27 February 2006
Zaha Hadid: Phaeno Science Centre
George L Legendre & Omar Al-Omari: Teacher/Student –
Not the Last Word
Exhibition openings

28 February 2006
Zaha Hadid
The Design of the Phaeno Centre, Wolfsburg
Evening lecture

2 March 2006
Hanif Kara
Christos Passas
Paul Scott
The Realisation of the Phaeno Centre, Wolfsburg
Roundtable discussion moderated by Mike Weinstock

March to May 2006
Monia De Marchi and Jon Cole
Precision Modelling with CNC
Saturday morning open Media Studies workshop

6 March 2006
Eric Owen Moss
In Sight of the Invisible
Evening lecture

6 March 2006
Scales and/of Engagement I
Architectural Urbanism, Social & Political Space (AUSP) Research Cluster open discussion with presentations by Intermediate 10, Diploma Units 2, 6, 10, 15, Housing & Urbanism and PhD programme

7 March 2006
George L-Legendre
Before and After: What a Mess
Evening lecture

7 March 2006
Bodyline: The End of Our Meta-Mechanical Body
Launch of new AA publication edited by George L Legendre

10 March 2006
Media Studies Day Exhibition

10 March 2006
Freetown Christiana
Informal presentations hosted by Inter 10 and AUSP

10 March 2006
Stefano Boeri
Hans Ulrich Obrist
Brett Steele
Journalism & Criticism – Architecture & Cities
Open discussion moderated by Shumon Basar and hosted by the AUSP Research Cluster

14 March 2006
Scales and/of Engagement II
Architectural Urbanism, Social & Political Space (AUSP) Research Cluster open discussion with presentations by Intermediate 10, Diploma 6 and Housing & Urbanism

14 March 2006
François Roche
R&Sie(n) Architects
Making With...
Evening lecture

15 March 2006
Architectural Residencies
Erland Blakstad Haffner
Clare Cumberlidge
Theo Lorenz
Frances Morrell
Barbara Stevini
Rob Wilson
Roundtable discussion hosted by Alternative Practices and Research Initiatives (APRI) Research Cluster

15 March 2006
Winka Dubbledam
From HardWare to SoftForm
Evening Lecture

16 March 2006
Techniques and Technologies in Morphogenetic Design
Christopher Hight
George Jeronimidis
Robert Aish
Hugh Whitehead
Michael Hensel
Achim Menges
AA/AD Design Symposium

17 March 2006
Differentiated Structures in Nature and Design
George Jeronimidis
Julian Vincent
Chris Williams
Mike Weinstock
Wolf Mangelsdorf
Michael Cook
Christopher Hight
Michael Hensel
Achim Menges
AA Symposium

20 March 2006
Michael Speaks
Liars, Bullshitters and Intelligencers
Evening lecture

21/22 March 2006
Michael Speaks
Design Intelligence: Thinking in Architecture after the End of Theory
Visiting theory seminars

23 March 2006
AAir Salon
Filter Feeder
Spectral sound

25/26 April 2006
Third Year Previews

27 April 2006
Spaghetti Structures
Annual First Year Structures competition

28 April 2006
The Thames Gateway Assembly at the AA
Every Little Helps
10 Lights: Inter 3
Unit Trip Sampler:
AA Student Forum
Lagos: Transient Realities
Exhibition openings

29 April 2006
Threshold Live:
Residency Exhibition
Volker Morawe and John Wynne with Diploma 9

3/4 May 2006
Fifth Year Previews

4 May 2006
Runzelstirn & Gurgelstock/ Schimpfluch-Gruppe
Performance presented by AA Independent Radio in association with Entr'acte, Harbinger Sound and the AA Student Forum

4 May 2006
Structure as Space: Architecture and Engineering in the Works of Jürg Conzett and His Partners
New AA Publication

5 May 2006
Jose Salinas
Finding Processes
Open seminar